HAS THE

TRIBULATION

BEGUN?

AMIR TSARFATI

HARVEST PROPHECY
AN IMPRINT OF HARVEST HOUSE PUBLISHERS

Cover design by Bryce Williamson

Cover photos © 4khz, Elena_Garder / Getty Images

Interior design by KUHN Design Group

For bulk, special sales, or ministry purchases, please call 1-800-547-8979.
Email: Customerservice@hhpbooks.com

This logo is a federally registered trademark of the Hawkins Children's LLC. Harvest House Publishers, Inc., is the exclusive licensee of this trademark.

Has the Tribulation Begun?
Copyright © 2023 by Amir Tsarfati
Published by Harvest House Publishers
Eugene, Oregon 97408
www.harvesthousepublishers.com

ISBN 978-0-7369-8726-4 (pbk.)
ISBN 978-0-7369-8727-1 (eBook)
Library of Congress Control Number: 2022945918

Printed in the United States of America

23 24 25 26 27 28 29 30 31 / BP / 10 9 8 7 6 5 4 3 2 1

I dedicate this book to all the faithful followers and supporters of Behold Israel. You have stayed with me through so much. Even as the attacks have come one after another, you have remained standing with me as biblically grounded voices of sound mind, love, and power. You have rejected all the sensationalism bought into by those who lack wisdom, character, and discernment, and instead, have chosen to submit yourselves to the leading of Scripture alone. I am blessed to have you as part of this ministry.

ACKNOWLEDGMENTS

First and foremost, I want to thank the Lord for His faithfulness throughout my life. Before I was even born, He loved me deeply and had a plan for my life. What a blessing it is to serve my Savior each and every day.

I want to thank Steve Yohn for his assistance in writing this book. I am so grateful for his ability to take my thoughts and put them down on paper.

I want to thank my wife, Miriam, my four children, and my daughter-in-law. Even through the hard times, we have remained strong as a family. I am so blessed to have you.

I want to thank my team at Behold Israel for their love, support, and dedication— Mike, H.T. and Tara, Gale and Florene, Donalee, Joanne, Nick and Tina, Jason, Abigail, Kayo, and Steve. You are the backbone of this ministry, and your commitment to follow God's will is what keeps us on the right track.

Special thanks to the many translators who have made my YouTube messages available in 20 different languages. Also, I offer great thanks to the many ministry coordinators around the globe who ensure everything runs smoothly at our conferences.

Thanks to Shane for his great work on our graphics and social media. Thanks to Jon for our excellent app and website. Thanks to Don at Veni Graphics for his excellent work. Also, thank you to the team at Tenfold BPO for all that you do.

Thank you to Bob Hawkins, Steve Miller, Kim Moore, and the wonderful team at Harvest House for all your hard work in making this book happen.

Finally, thank you so much to the hundreds of thousands of followers, prayer partners, and ministry supporters of Behold Israel. This ministry would not exist without you.

CONTENTS

1

HAS THE
TRIBULATION BEGUN?

No.

Calm down. Breathe deep. You heard me right. The tribulation has not begun.

"But, Amir, look at the world around us! Political chaos, financial meltdowns, rampant immorality! Surely this must be the tribulation!"

No, it is not.

"The world is overheating in the summers and freezing in the winters. There are global pandemics and devastating earthquakes. There is war in Europe and constant conflict in the Middle East and Asia and all over the world. Technology has gotten to the point that they are starting to microchip people. Are you blind?"

It's true that without my glasses my sight may be a bit iffy. But I am not blind, and the answer is still no. One hundred percent, unequivocally, without a doubt, the tribulation has not begun.

How can I be so confident? Quite simply, it's because my focus is not on the world, but in the Word. The Bible makes it clear that what we are experiencing now is a firecracker compared to the nuclear weapon of the tribulation. My advice for those who do not follow Jesus Christ is to enjoy the good times now; they're not going to last.

There you go. You're welcome. You can relax once again.

I recognize that from a literary standpoint, I have just committed a cardinal sin. In what might be a compositional record, I answered the propositional question of this entire work in the first word of the book. I solved the mystery before anyone even knew there had been a crime. It's like Agatha Christie or Arthur Conan Doyle beginning one of their great who-dun-it novels with the line "The butler did it." I have just spoiler-alerted the title of my book into oblivion.

But before you put this book back on the shelf with a contented, "Well, that was easy," let me tell you that there is a method to my madness. There are much deeper and more important issues at play here than simply the timing of the tribulation. Timing is the easy part. Certainly, I could have left the question "Has the tribulation begun?" hanging throughout the entire book, building the suspense chapter by chapter, creating concern and fear in your minds. But that would just be sensationalism. I would be playing with your emotions. Easy questions demand easy answers. Here, the easy answer is "No, the tribulation has not begun." In subsequent chapters, I'll fill you in on why I can so adamantly make that statement, why it is so important to understand the tribulation, and how you can know that the tribulation has actually begun should you happen to still be around when it launches.

There is one more even greater goal for this book. Early in the life of the church in Thessaloniki, the people were asking much the same question that we are answering in this book. Rumors were circulating that the end-times scenario had kicked off. The members of this church didn't know what to believe. That's when Paul stepped in, writing, "Now, brethren, concerning the coming of our Lord Jesus Christ and our gathering together to Him, we ask you, not to be soon shaken in mind or troubled, either by spirit or by word or by letter, as if from us, as though the day of Christ had come" (2 Thessalonians 2:1-2). The apostle then proceeded to teach them and remind them of what he had said in the past, easing their troubled minds.

When you are done with this book, I want you to be able to do the exact same thing with your loved ones, your friends, your fellow church members—anyone who needs to be comforted with the truth. My goal is for you to be equipped to be able to explain to anyone why this cannot possibly be the tribulation, how they can know the signs that the actual tribulation has begun, and how they can ensure that they won't be around to experience it.

IT'S NOT SO BAD

A primary theme through Paul's second letter to the Corinthians is perspective. He constantly returned to the idea that we need to look at the temporary nature of this life through the lens of eternity. In the fourth chapter, he wrote:

> Our light affliction, which is but for a moment, is working for us a far more exceeding and eternal weight of glory, while we do not look at the things which are seen, but at the things which are not seen. For the things which are seen are temporary, but the things which are not seen are eternal (2 Corinthians 4:17-18).

The apostle, who himself knew great suffering through his life, wrote that no matter what it is you are going through, it is really nothing when you look at it in God's big picture. That can be a jarring assertion to hear, particularly if you are dealing with a chronic issue. The woman with multiple sclerosis, the man with ALS, the young adult with cerebral palsy—doubtless your life feels like anything other than a "light affliction." But Paul's encouragement is "Just wait and see what God has planned for you. When compared with the exceeding and eternal weight of the glory of God—experiencing the beauty and joy of being in His incomparable presence—the pain of these earthly days will seem like nothing."

The opposite is true when it comes to the tribulation. Once those seven years begin, the troubles of our current situation will also seem like "light affliction." However, it will not be because life will become so much better. Instead, people will long for the tranquil days of mask mandates and government overreach and wars in countries not their own. "Remember when the government closed all our businesses and shut down our churches? Oh, life was so much easier then."

This is not to downplay anything that has been happening recently. These have been difficult times. This is particularly true for those of you in America. I am not from the United States, so I can speak as someone who is looking in from the outside. Those of you reading this who are Americans have been raised expecting the ideals of life, liberty, and the pursuit of happiness. You hold on to them as your birthrights—your "inalienable rights"—and you say that you will fight to the death to maintain them. And, up until now, you've done an excellent job of doing so.

That's why everybody wants to come to America. Whether legally or illegally, the United States is the world's immigration capital. With 50.6 million foreign-born residents, you have over three times more than the second-place country.[1] And with good reason—America is a great place to live. People don't risk their life or livelihood to leave their country and go to one that's worse. They go to a place that's a step up. They travel to a new land that will give more opportunity for themselves and for their children. So much of that is based on those American ideals of life, liberty, and the pursuit of happiness.

In Europe, people don't have those same ideals. In the Middle East, they're not part of our mindset. Go to Afghanistan to pursue your rights of life, liberty, and the pursuit of happiness, and your head will be rolling down the aisle. In the rest of the world, we are used to government overreach. We expect our rights to occasionally get trampled on. We don't like it, but it's the nature of things. Now, you in America are experiencing this for the first time. You're saying,

"What's going on? They're changing the rules! They're going beyond their constitutional mandates!" And the rest of us in the world are saying, "Welcome to the club, Yanks!"

And because I have the gift of encouragement, I will say to those of you in America and the rest of the world, "It's only going to get worse!" There you go! *Mazel tov!*

THE SCRIPTURES AND THE POWER OF GOD

In the week before His crucifixion, Jesus had a confrontation with the Sadducees. The Sadducees were a sect of Judaism that did not believe in the resurrection of the dead. Once your ticket was punched, it remained punched. Dead meant dead. They approached Jesus with a question that was a true "gotcha." They had probably used it many times throughout the years, honing it to perfection. Now, they were going to thrust this sharpened theological dagger at this backwoods country preacher from Nazareth, of all places, so they could send Him scurrying back to whatever rock He crawled out from under.

> Teacher, Moses said that if a man dies, having no children, his brother shall marry his wife and raise up offspring for his brother. Now there were with us seven brothers. The first died after he had married, and having no offspring, left his wife to his brother. Likewise the second also, and the third, even to the seventh. Last of all the woman died also. Therefore, in the resurrection, whose wife of the seven will she be? For they all had her (Matthew 22:24-28).

You can hear the smugness in their tone, starting out with what for them was probably a very sarcastic "Teacher." No one else had ever been able to satisfactorily answer this doctrinal brain twister. Certainly, this bumpkin didn't stand a chance.

Jesus' answer was exquisite.

"You are mistaken, not knowing the Scriptures nor the power of God" (v. 29).

Jesus said to these self-important religious teachers, "Have you never even read your Bibles? Obviously not. And because you don't know God's Word, you don't know God." He went on to prove His authority to call them out by explaining familial relationships in heaven and proving that there is life after death—all in four sentences. The crowds were astonished, and the Sadducees were silenced.

The deficiencies for which Jesus called out these religious leaders are the same ones that are causing people today to ask whether we are in the tribulation. Too many inside and outside of the church don't know God's Word and, therefore, don't know God. This biblical illiteracy opens the hearts of many to fear and their ears to the rampant sensationalism that has permeated the Christian airwaves and social media.

Deception is rampant and so many in the church are caught up in the lies because they are desperate for that one special insight, that next hidden mystery. Our "bigger and better" society craves the tidbits of information that lift an individual to an elite status of being "in the know," while the rest of those poor saps in the church are still holding on to those old, simple beliefs. Where once a believer was content with the words written on the pages of their Bibles, now they have the online preacher who unlocks the code and gives them the "words behind the words," the secret meanings, the obscure cultural insights. I can't tell you how many times someone has wanted to explain to me, a Jerusalem-born Jew, the deeper meanings of the Old Testament Hebrew. I tell them, "Uh, you do know who I am and where I live, don't you?"

But it is those little presuppositional nuggets that the Scripture-twisting teachers use to make claims like, "The Bible said, 'But of that day and hour no one knows,' but I've figured out the timing!"

Or, "When Jesus said, 'I will come again and receive you to Myself; that where I am, there you may be also,' He really meant, 'I will come again for you to receive Me to yourselves; that where you are, I may be also.'"

Or, even, "When Paul wrote, 'Has God cast away His people [Israel]? Certainly not!' he actually meant, 'You're darn tootin' He did!'"

When biblical interpretation moves from "What does the Bible say?" to "What does the Bible *really* say?" you're in for trouble. Of course, there are times when historical culture is relevant and figures of speech and symbolism come into play. But those are typically very clear when being employed. Anything else is deception. And it is biblical illiteracy and the resultant lack of understanding of who God is and how He operates that makes so many in the church susceptible to the current rampant mishandling of the Scripture.

TRUTHS BEING TARGETED BY SATAN

Satan is the great deceiver, and by *great*, I mean that he's really good at his job. As I look at the madness of this world and the ineffectiveness of the church to be able to address it, I see six biblical truths the enemy is undermining to create his chaos.

Targeted Truth 1: Jesus alone is the Life, the Truth, and the Way to God.

Jesus is the only way to the Father, the only true answer to sin's problem, the only source of eternal life. How do we know this? He testified to it Himself. "Jesus said to him, 'I am the way, the truth, and the life. No one comes to the Father except through Me'" (John 14:6). Many focus on the exclusivity of the first half of Jesus' statement, but it is the second sentence that slams the door on every other belief system. "No one" means no one! No person on planet Earth can ever come to the Father except through Jesus.

Some accuse Christians of being uncaring or unsympathetic. It is a bigoted, exclusionary, arrogant statement to say that you are right and everyone else is wrong. But I'm not saying that I'm right. Jesus is! This isn't what Amir thinks; it's what the Lord said. So, don't try to turn Jesus into an open-armed, universalist, save-everybody-no-matter-what-they-believe-because-He's-just-so-darn-loving kind of person. You cannot believe in Jesus while not believing in what He said. And what Jesus said is that salvation is found in Him and nowhere else.

It's not just Jesus who said that He is the only way. While speaking of Him, Peter the disciple said to the Jewish religious leaders, "Nor is there salvation in any other, for there is no other name under heaven given among men by which we must be saved" (Acts 4:12). The apostle Paul, writing to Gentiles in Rome, asserted, "If you confess with your mouth the Lord Jesus and believe in your heart that God has raised Him from the dead, you will be saved. For with the heart one believes unto righteousness, and with the mouth confession is made unto salvation" (Romans 10:9-10). Confess Jesus with your mouth and believe in your heart. That's the only way.

By the way, did you know that in Islam, if you were drunk and someone told you to say, "*Allahu akbar*," which means "God is greatest," three times and you did so, you would automatically become a Muslim? "*Allahu akbar, Allahu akbar, Allahu akbar*"—boom—that's all it takes to make Allah happy. If you sober up the next day and decide you don't want to be a Muslim, tough luck. If you leave now, it's apostasy.

That kind of mindless, heartless salvation formula is why Paul wrote the two-part presentation found in Romans. Confess Jesus with your mouth and believe in your heart. That's what brings the transformation. This is not religion; it is not ritual. This is faith. And today, it is under attack, even by people who call themselves Christians. A 2008 Pew Research Center survey found that 52 percent of all Americans who profess to be Christians believe that numerous other belief systems can lead to eternal life.[2] How can anyone who "knows the Scriptures and the power of God" hold to that deception?

This move toward ecumenism is directly from the enemy, and it fits right into his ultimate goal of there being one world religion during the tribulation. In February 2019, Pope Francis traveled to Abu Dhabi, UAE, where he met with Grand Imam of Al-Azhar Ahmed Al-Tayyeb. Together they signed a document that invited "all persons who have faith in God and faith in *human fraternity* to unite and work together so that it may serve as a guide for future generations to advance a culture of mutual respect in the awareness of the great divine grace that makes all human beings brothers and sisters."[3] Included in the statement was the call for "intellectuals, philosophers, religious figures, artists, media professionals and men and women of culture in every part of the world, to rediscover the values of peace, justice, goodness, beauty, human fraternity and coexistence in order to confirm the importance of these values as anchors of salvation for all, and to promote them everywhere."[4] You want to anchor your salvation? You just have to be a good person with the good values of peace, justice, beauty, fraternity, and coexistence. This is the new religion; it just doesn't have a name yet.

This religious gobbledygook is meaningless. It is salvation determined by one's values. But our eternity is not based on the goodness in our hearts or the nice things we do. The disciple John made the source of our salvation very clear when he wrote, "God has given us eternal life, and this life is in His Son. He who has the Son has life; he who does not have the Son of God does not have life" (1 John 5:11-12). Our hope is built on Jesus Christ, and Jesus Christ alone. A pope may tell the world, "Those who have chosen the way of the Gospel Beatitudes and live as 'the poor in spirit,' detached from material goods, in order to raise up the lowly of the earth from the dust of their humiliation, will enter the kingdom of God."[5] But Scripture says that it is those who choose the way of the gospel of Jesus Christ who will enter the kingdom of God, and then the life of the Beatitudes will follow.

Again, Satan is very good at what he does. When he deceives, he does so using the words that he knows people want to hear. This has always been true. God said of the people of Judah, "The prophets prophesy falsely, and the priests rule by their own power; and My people love to have it so" (Jeremiah 5:31). People love to hear religious-sounding talk, but they hold a caveat. They will listen as long as it is anything but the convicting words of God that ask them to believe in Jesus and make Him their Lord because He has already carried out the work of salvation on the cross. They don't want to hear about repentance or sin. They don't want to talk about holiness. "Instead, won't you please tell me about how I can be good, fulfill myself in this world, and live my best life now?"

This ties in hand in hand with the coming of the lawless one. He will know exactly what the people of this world will want. He will come to the fore with signs and lying wonders. His words will tickle the world's receptive ears. People will perish because they preferred lies to the truth. They will be very content to believe that Jesus is *a way*. Just don't tell them that He is *the Way*.

Targeted Truth 2: All people are born sinners.

"Amir, who are you to call me a sinner? Sure, I may occasionally commit minor offenses, engage in small peccadillos, participate in slightly naughty behavior, and indulge in somewhat questionable activities. But a sinner? Take the log out of your own eye, mister, before you judge me!"

Trust me, my friend, I am fully aware of my own indiscretions. I am also cognizant of the fact that those activities make me a full-fledged sinner. And I am not the one who has given you that same designation—God is.

> If we say that we have no sin, we deceive ourselves, and the truth is not in us…If we say that we have not sinned, we make Him a liar, and His word is not in us (1 John 1:8, 10).

However, to call someone a sinner today is said to be rude and hurtful. It's hate speech. Isn't one person's sin simply another person's lifestyle choice? This attitude is all part of the enemy's plan to de-sinify sin. Once sin is marginalized, confined to only the biggies like murder and sexual abuse and calling people by the wrong pronouns, then humanity no longer has a sin problem to deal with. The cross of Jesus is unnecessary. There is nothing separating us from God.

But the Bible makes it clear that every one of us has a sin problem. Paul wrote, "Through one man sin entered the world, and death through sin, and thus death spread to all men, because all sinned" (Romans 5:12). Sin may have entered the world through one man, but every one of us has jumped on the sin bandwagon. And if you have sinned, you are, by definition, a sinner. When David was nailed by Nathan the prophet for his affair with Bathsheba, he admitted, "Behold, I was brought forth in iniquity, and in sin my mother conceived me" (Psalm 51:5). We were born with sin. That's why we need to be born again. We must be born from above in order to remove the sin taint.

As we saw in the passage from John's letter, if we say we have no sin, we are deceiving ourselves. That is the deception that Satan is spreading. "Don't worry. You're fine. You may slip up every now and then, but are you a sinner? Nah. Just relax, breathe deep, and let your conscience be your guide."

Targeted Truth 3: Israel is still God's chosen people and can't be replaced.

So many people are walking around in churches today saying that Israel is no longer God's people. He turned His back on them because they turned their backs on Him. Just like when your child, in anger, says, "I hate you," you automatically hate them back, right? Wrong. But that is the kind of thin-skinned petulance that Replacement Theology followers seem to ascribe to God. He is a reactive Father whose love for us is wholly dependent upon our actions toward Him.

"Wait a minute, Amir. Didn't you already write a whole book about this called *Israel and the Church*? And you're still harping on it?" Yes, I did, and thank you for reading it. And yes, I am still harping on it because it is such a critical doctrine for understanding the character of God and for figuring out the end times, particularly the tribulation.

That is why the enemy is attacking this truth so diligently. God is not a user. He didn't choose Israel for a time only to later say, "Sorry, I've found somebody younger and prettier." The gap between the Old Testament and New Testament was not God's mid-life crisis. He made it very clear that He would never abandon His chosen people. Through Jeremiah, He said,

> If you can break My covenant with the day and My covenant with the night, so that there will not be day and night in their season, then My covenant may also be broken with David My servant, so that he shall not have a son to reign on his throne, and with the Levites, the priests, My ministers. As the host of heaven cannot be numbered, nor the sand of the sea measured, so will I multiply the descendants of David My servant and the Levites who minister to Me (Jeremiah 33:20-22).

A few verses later, God reiterated this commitment:

> If My covenant is not with day and night, and if I have not appointed the ordinances of heaven and earth, then I will cast away the descendants of Jacob and David My servant, so that I will not take any of his descendants to be rulers over the descendants of Abraham, Isaac, and Jacob. For I will cause their captives to return, and will have mercy on them (vv. 25-26).

Think about that. He's saying, "As long as the moon is there and the sun is there and the stars are there, Israel will still be my people." That's why I tell the ayatollahs in Iran, "When you finally get your nuke, aim it at the sun. Because only when it is gone will Israel no longer exist." The sole way to say that these words in Jeremiah are not promising a lasting Israel is to claim that the church is now Israel, which is what the Replacement folk do. But read those passages again. What kind of mental gymnastics do you need to go through to turn those extremely Jewish passages into promises to the church?

If God is done with the Jews, then there is no need for a tribulation to discipline His people. If there is no need for a tribulation, then there is no need for a rapture to remove the church from God's coming wrath because there will be no coming wrath. If there is no rapture and no tribulation, what reason is there for a literal millennium? After all, there will be no need to restore God's original creation under the earthly rule of Jesus from Jerusalem. This is how we end up with amillennialism and postmillennialism.

Unfortunately for those who hold to those beliefs, we find all those pesky little passages in 1 Thessalonians and 1 Corinthians and the Gospel of John that talk about the rapture. There's the book of Revelation, which spends a lot of time detailing the events and the timeline of the tribulation. There are many passages throughout the Scriptures, particularly in Isaiah and Revelation, that highlight a 1,000-year reign of Christ. The only way to get around those parts of Scripture is to allegorize them and say that they don't really say what it looks like they say. When the church buys into that, then the enemy's deception about Israel is complete.

Targeted Truth 4: In order to be prepared, we must know the times and the seasons.

One of the enemy's greatest victories has been convincing so many pastors and Christian leaders that Bible prophecy is irrelevant to the church today. "There are tons of more practical subjects to preach on. Topics that affect real life," they say. As a result, most Christians are clueless about the incredible extent to which God has moved forward on His end-times plan. As for practicality, how is it possible to discern the events taking place in our crazy world without having a biblical lens through which to examine them?

In July 2022, a very interesting meeting took place. It was a trilateral summit held in Tehran and attended by Iranian President Ebrahim Raisi, Russian President Vladimir Putin, and Turkish President Recep Tayyip Erdogan. Another way to look at it is that it was an alliance-forming gathering of a radical terrorist regime, a belligerent expansionist nation, and a member of NATO, an organization that was created to stand up against that belligerent expansionist nation.

Strange bedfellows? Maybe to some. But what makes no sense to many fits right into Bible prophecy. Both Turkey and Iran are listed amongst the allies of Rosh (Russia) in Ezekiel 38.

> Son of man, set your face against Gog, of the land of Magog, the prince of Rosh, Meshech, and Tubal, and prophesy against him, and say, "Thus says the Lord God: 'Behold, I *am* against you, O Gog, the prince of Rosh, Meshech, and Tubal. I will turn you around, put hooks into your jaws, and lead you out, with all your army, horses, and horsemen, all splendidly clothed, a great company with bucklers and shields, all of them handling swords. Persia, Ethiopia, and Libya are with them, all of them with shield and helmet; Gomer and all its troops; the house of Togarmah from the far north and all its troops—many people are with you'" (vv. 2-6).

Persia is Iran, and Gomer and the house of Togarmah are Turkey. Soon, they will together attempt to invade Israel, only to be destroyed by God.

Therefore, son of man, prophesy and say to Gog, "Thus says the Lord GOD: 'On that day when My people Israel dwell safely, will you not know it? Then you will come from your place out of the far north, you and many peoples with you, all of them riding on horses, a great company and a mighty army. You will come up against My people Israel like a cloud, to cover the land. It will be in the latter days that I will bring you against My land, so that the nations may know Me, when I am hallowed in you, O Gog, before their eyes…I will call for a sword against Gog throughout all My mountains,' says the Lord GOD. 'Every man's sword will be against his brother. And I will bring him to judgment with pestilence and bloodshed; I will rain down on him, on his troops, and on the many peoples who *are* with him, flooding rain, great hailstones, fire, and brimstone. Thus I will magnify Myself and sanctify Myself, and I will be known in the eyes of many nations. Then they shall know that I am the LORD'" (vv. 14-16, 21-23).

These three world leaders likely have no clue about the part their countries will play in God's plan. But Ezekiel makes it clear that there will come a day when the people of Israel will be back in their land and thriving. It is at that time that this evil alliance will attack. All one needs to do is look at how wealthy and powerful Israel has become to know that the season is ripe for these events.

This is also the time and season for the beginnings of a one-world government. For a global government to replace national governments, the national governments must disappoint the citizenry. This morning as I am writing this, not an hour ago, the US Supreme Court overturned the *Roe v. Wade* abortion decision. Liberals of the nation are promising serious repercussions in the months ahead.

Add to that, the increasing political unrest, international conflicts, rampant inflation, droughts, and other natural disasters across the globe. Whereas others see the world adrift in a sea of chaos, Christians who know Scripture and the power of God recognize these as the birth pangs promised by Jesus when He was speaking to His disciples on the Mount of Olives. He said,

> You will hear of wars and rumors of wars. See that you are not troubled; for all these things must come to pass, but the end is not yet. For nation will rise against nation, and kingdom against kingdom. And there will be famines, pestilences, and earthquakes in various places. All these are the beginning of sorrows (Matthew 24:6-8).

We who are Christians should not be surprised by what we see. Not only do we know that these difficult times are coming; we know that they must come. Why? Because God has already seen it happening. He is above time. That's why He said, "I am God, and there is no other; I am God, and there is none like Me, declaring the end from the beginning, and from ancient times things that are not yet done" (Isaiah 46:9-10). He knows what is going to happen. He is not watching Eastern Europe and wondering, *Will it be Russia or Ukraine who wins?* He knows all that is going to happen, and all that happens will do so according to His will.

That is why a book written 2,000 years ago can give us insight as to what is going on today. The Bible will not go out of date because it is a timeless message from a timeless God. When Israel celebrated its sixtieth anniversary in 2008, I visited the Israel Museum, where they were showing an authentic Isaiah scroll from 2,200–2,300 years ago. I had my Hebrew Bible open as I read the words on that scroll. You know what? They matched! The Bible has not and will not change. If you are looking to make sense of the world around you—to understand the times and seasons—don't turn to Facebook or YouTube. Dr. Google does not have an advanced-enough degree. The only place you will find truth 100 percent of the time is in the Word of God.

Targeted Truth 5: When Jesus returns, we need to be found doing the Father's business.

When I was in the military, we would occasionally have barracks inspections. Typically, these were unannounced. Why? Because our superiors knew that if they told us there would be an inspection every Thursday at 10:00 a.m., then Friday through Wednesday the barracks would be a mess. Then, Thursday at 9:00 a.m., we would have one hour of panicked cleaning so that all would be spotless for the review. Instead, in their great wisdom, they left the timing of the inspections ambiguous so that we always had to have everything perfect and ready for scrutiny. This preparedness is what Jesus was speaking of when He said,

> Let your waist be girded and your lamps burning; and you yourselves be like men who wait for their master, when he will return from the wedding, that when he comes and knocks they may open to him immediately. Blessed are those servants whom the master, when he comes, will find watching. Assuredly, I say to you that he will gird himself and have them sit down to eat, and will come and serve them (Luke 12:35-37).

Unfortunately, if Jesus were to return today, He would not find His church ready. He would find His church distracted. Rather than teaching the Word of God, too many pastors are preaching sensationalism. Topical clickbait sermons are widespread, particularly when it comes to COVID. "The vaccine is the mark of the beast," they announce, causing panic and division within their congregations. "Take it and you are irretrievably bound for hell." Believe me, there is a lot to criticize about the vaccines, but it is not the mark of the beast. Will the church even be around for the mark of the beast? Absolutely not.

I have even read of pastors saying that the coronavirus is tied into the work of the first rider of the apocalypse.

> Now I saw when the Lamb opened one of the seals; and I heard one of the four living creatures saying with a voice like thunder, "Come and see." And I looked, and behold, a white horse. He who sat on it had a bow; and a crown was given to him, and he went out conquering and to conquer (Revelation 6:1-2).

You saw it there, didn't you? Plain as the nose on your face. The rider is wearing a crown. The word *corona* means "crown." Boom! Proof positive right in the text. That same logic also led me to discover that since Corona is the name of a beer, the rider's saddle likely sported a drink holder. There's got to be some deep theological truth in that tidbit too.

This kind of irresponsible, unbiblical teaching is causing so much fear and division in the church. Love and Christlike compassion for one another has been replaced in many circles by vicious attacks over mandates and vaccines. My heart broke when I read this *New York Post* headline: "Pastor threatens to kick out mask-wearing worshippers from church."[6] Can you imagine Jesus getting up in the front of a synagogue and saying, "You, in the yarmulke, you think that will save you? Get out of here! And you with the phylacteries, take a hike!" What are we turning our churches into?

Satan is gaining victory after victory as the church becomes more divided than ever. What's sad is that frequently, people are battling over issues that don't pertain to salvation. Jesus laid out a mandate for His disciples when He said, "A new commandment I give to you, that you love one another; as I have loved you, that you also love one another. By this all will know that you are My disciples, if you have love for one another" (John 13:34-35). Jesus had plenty to disagree with when it came to the attitudes and actions of His disciples. Still, He loved them sacrificially, and He told them that they must have that same kind of love for one another.

In the church, we are each other's "one anothers." We may not always agree when it comes to certain issues, be they doctrinal, political, or social. However, we do agree on the gospel, and we are all striving to be led by the Holy Spirit in righteousness and holiness. That must unite us together, and it must unite us now! We cannot wait until ten minutes before inspection to clean up our act. We must be about the Father's gospel business today and every day until our Savior returns to take us to be with Him.

Targeted Truth 6: Believers will be raptured before the tribulation.

So many pastors have bought into the deception that there is no rapture of the church, and they are teaching that belief to their congregations. Confidently, they hold up their Bibles and announce, "The word *rapture* isn't even found in this book." And to a degree, they're right! But neither is the word *replacement*—just saying.

I've got news for the naysayers: *rapture* is in the Bible. It's just not in your English Bible. The New Testament was written in Greek, and one of the words used was *harpazo*, which you'll typically find translated as "caught up" or "caught away." When the Greek New Testament was translated into Latin, this word became *rapturo*, which is where we get the word *rapture*. So, when people say, "Paul didn't believe in a rapture. Neither did Jesus," my response is the same one that Jesus gave to the Sadducees: "You obviously don't know the Scriptures or the power of God." We'll get into more detail about this in a later chapter.

This lack of belief in a rapture is so sad because it steals away one of the great hopes of the Bible. The strength of this deception is so great that some people appear to be hoping that there will be no rapture, as if avoiding the horrors of the tribulation would be a terrible thing. A number of years back, a blogger dropped a post called "9 Reasons We Can Be Confident Christians Won't Be Raptured Before the Tribulation."[7] It was, at its core, a summary of an article by a well-known and highly respected theologian[8] as to why we can rest easy that we'll get to enjoy firsthand God's wrath upon His creation. Phew, what a relief! I really wanted to see what a 100-pound hailstone looks like!

But we are not destined for the wrath of God. If you want to go through the tribulation, have at it. Just remember to stretch your neck out so your executioners get a clean shot. And it's not that I'm desperate to conjure up a reason why I don't have to endure the horrors of those tragic years. My hope doesn't come from devising some outlandish interpretation or uncovering hidden meanings in the biblical text. My hope comes from Paul's words—he wrote very clearly, "God did not appoint us to wrath, but to obtain salvation through our Lord Jesus Christ, who died for us, that whether we wake or sleep, we should live together with Him. Therefore comfort each other and edify one another, just as you also are doing" (1 Thessalonians 5:9-12). No wrath for the Lord's church. That's as comforting as a warm sheep's wool blanket on a damp winter's night.

DEEP-SEATED DECEPTION

Truth is under assault. Satan has already garnered a tremendous victory in the world through his lies. Sadly, he also has a foothold in the church, which continues to strengthen. Will his deceptions ever end? Thankfully, they will. John wrote:

> I saw an angel coming down from heaven, having the key to the bottomless pit and a great chain in his hand. He

laid hold of the dragon, that serpent of old, who is the Devil and Satan, and bound him for a thousand years; and he cast him into the bottomless pit, and shut him up, and set a seal on him, so that he should deceive the nations no more till the thousand years were finished. But after these things he must be released for a little while (Revelation 20:1-3).

There will come a time when the devil will be shut up so that he can't deceive anymore. His deceptions, however, are so ingrained in this fallen world that he doesn't need to be present for his influence to spread. Even during the idealistic period of Christ's reign on the earth when Satan is held captive, corrupted flesh will continue to corrupt souls. When Satan is finally released, he will find a populace ready and willing to follow his lead. If the deception will continue to be so strong when he is bound, imagine its power when he once again has free reign.

But before we get to that 1,000-year period of Satan being bound in the abyss, the world must undergo a seven-year period of God's wrath. No, the tribulation has not begun, but by all evidence, it is close. How can we know that? What will it look like when it comes? Both are good questions. But before we can determine the *what* of the tribulation, we need to examine its *why*. That is what the next chapter is all about.

THE TROUBLE
WITH JACOB

You sit with your spouse in the sunlight waiting for the ceremony to begin. Up front, the *chuppah* is beautifully adorned with large bouquets of white and yellow flowers and hanging greenery. Above is draped an intricately patterned silk cloth, creating the marriage canopy.

When you received the invitation from Yonatan and Anat, there had been a moment of hesitation. It had been several years since you last saw them. But after a little back-and-forth discussion that had begun with "Do we really want to go?," the two of you settled on "Well, we really should."

On the big day, the folding chairs were all occupied, and you looked at your watch. It was five minutes past the set time, but before you could begin to grumble, you remembered your own wedding, when you made your guests wait fifteen minutes for some last-minute dress issues. This was a time for celebration, and with celebration should come grace.

The music changed and the procession began. The rabbi led the wedding party, followed by the groomsmen. However, when Yonatan's parents walked past your seat, there was no Yonatan. That was certainly odd. Now, the bridesmaids began to slowly stroll down the aisle. They were followed by a little boy and a slightly older girl, the boy carrying a small pillow and the girl dropping flower petals.

Finally, the moment came for the arrival of the bride. You turned toward the back as you stood, only to be met by a most unexpected sight. Anat's parents were walking down the aisle alone.

No groom. No bride. What in the world was going on? Confused, you turned to the person next to you.

"Do you know what's happening? Where are Yonatan and Anat?" you asked.

"Oh, they broke up months ago. But weddings are such wonderful occasions that the rest of the family decided to hold it anyway."

A wedding with no bride and no groom. How does that make any sense? You can call it an ornately decorated outdoor gathering. You can call it a pre-cake eating service. But you can't call it a wedding. The whole purpose of a wedding is the uniting of a man and a woman in matrimony. No man and woman, no matrimony, no wedding.

When it comes to the tribulation, there is one essential party. Without this group, there is no tribulation. The whole horrific period is for their benefit—and, yes, I intentionally used the word *benefit*. Who is this necessary participant? In this case, contrary to the belief of many, it is not a bride. Instead, we can find the tribulation's essential party in the name that Jeremiah gives to this period of testing and wrath:

> Alas! For that day is great,
> so that none is like it;
> and it is the time of Jacob's trouble,
> but he shall be saved out of it (Jeremiah 30:7).

The prophet called the seven-year tribulation "Jacob's trouble." And who is this Jacob who has such a terrible target on his back? For this, we go back to the patriarchs. Jacob, a grandson of Abraham, physically wrestled with God in human form one night. God took him to the ground with a hip displacement, then said to him:

> "What *is* your name?"
>
> He said, "Jacob."
>
> And He said, "Your name shall no longer be called Jacob, but Israel; for you have struggled with God and with men, and have prevailed" (Genesis 32:27-28).

Jacob is Israel. Jacob's trouble is Israel's trouble. It is for Israel that the tribulation has been designed. Yes, there will be wrath upon the unbelieving world for their rejection of God and His free gift of salvation. But Jeremiah does not call this terrible time "global trouble" or "world trouble," or even "unbelievers' trouble." This period is directed toward Jacob with the purpose of bringing the Jewish people to the point that they are ready to accept the Messiah they have rejected. It is then at the end of the trouble that, as Paul wrote, "All Israel will be saved" (Romans 11:26).

For us to understand the tribulation, we must first understand Israel. What has God done with the nation in the past, what is He doing with it now, and what will He do with His chosen people in the future? Then, to get a complete picture, we must also investigate how the enemy is attacking Israel, how the world deals with Israel, and how the church must treat the nation and its people.

GOD AND ISRAEL

Israel is an intentional creation of God. It is not a group of people who happened to settle in the same area, band together, create a mini-civilization, and decide to call themselves Israel. God chose a man, then made a promise to him that out of his body would come a mighty nation.

Now the LORD had said to Abram:

"Get out of your country,
from your family
and from your father's house,
to a land that I will show you.

I will make you a great nation;
I will bless you
and make your name great;
and you shall be a blessing.

I will bless those who bless you,
and I will curse him who curses you;
and in you all the families of the earth shall be blessed"
(Genesis 12:1-3).

Notice that there was a purpose to God's creation of this nation. Israel wasn't formed just so that these people could have some sort of spiritual superiority. The nation of Israel was designed to be a blessing to the whole world. Were the Jews given a special relationship with God? You bet. But with great privilege comes great responsibility. They were to reflect the glory of God to the rest of the world. Israel was to be God's ambassador on this earth. Unfortunately, over the millennia, we Jews have done very well at expressing our great privilege, and less so at carrying out our great responsibility.

But as poorly as Israel has done at living up to their end of the covenant with God, God has perfectly upheld His end of the bargain. His promise to Abraham did not come with an expiration date. There were no terms to it. All the active parts of the covenant began with "I will" and were said by God. It is because of this loving permanent promise that the time of Jacob's trouble is coming. The Lord is seeking not to destroy the Jews, but to bring them back to the original close relationship that He had with the patriarchs. Through the prophet Hosea, God said this about His future restoration plan:

> I will return again to My place
> till they acknowledge their offense.
> Then they will seek My face;
> in their affliction they will earnestly seek Me (5:15).

So often it takes affliction to bring us to God. I suppose it speaks to the stubbornness of us Jews that it takes tribulation-level affliction to get us to earnestly seek the Lord. How amazing is it that when my people do come looking for God, He will be there waiting for them with open arms! That is true for all of us, Jew and Gentile alike, when we turn to Him.

Not only is Israel an intentional creation, but it is also a miraculous creation. From the beginning, God made sure that it was evident to all that this group of people existed because of Him and no one else. If Abraham and Sarah had been two young adults in their mid-twenties, the birth of Isaac would have been nothing special. Instead, God chose a path that would force everyone to recognize that His hand was in it. The plan was so unusual and unexpected that Abraham couldn't keep a straight face when he heard it. "Abraham fell on his face and laughed, and said in his heart, 'Shall a child be born to a man who is one hundred years old? And shall Sarah, who is ninety years old, bear a child?'" (Genesis 17:17). Yet that is exactly what happened. Only God, by an act of His will, could have launched the Jewish nation through two people whose combined ages neared the bicentennial mark. And time and again through the ages, He has miraculously kept the nation of Israel alive.

Rarely has the hand of God been so evident on the nation of Israel as it is today. Before the Jews returned, the region was just barren wasteland. But long ago, God had spoken through the prophet

Ezekiel, "You, O mountains of Israel, you shall shoot forth your branches and yield your fruit to My people Israel, for they are about to come" (36:8). On my many flights, one event is consistent. As we near our destination, the pilot will say over the speakers, "In preparation for landing, please buckle your seat belts." In Ezekiel, God said, "In preparation for the return of My people, land spring up and be fruitful."

This is exactly what happened in the years leading up to Israel becoming a nation again in 1948. And it is what continues to take place today. If you have ever been to Israel, you know its bounty. Just the breakfast there—the fruits and vegetables—it's unbelievable. I've travelled all over, likely to your country, and I'm sorry to say, you folk are all missing out.

Once the land was prepared to receive its former inhabitants, God miraculously brought back the people, just as He had promised:

> "I will sanctify My great name, which has been profaned among the nations, which you have profaned in their midst; and the nations shall know that I am the LORD," says the Lord GOD, "when I am hallowed in you before their eyes. For I will take you from among the nations, gather you out of all countries, and bring you into your own land" (Ezekiel 36:23-24).

Whose land were they going to come back to? Is it the Palestinians' land? Is it the Arabs' land? Is it the British Mandate? No, God said they would return to "your own land." And once God started the flow of people, no one could stop it. My mother was born in a detention camp on the island of Cyprus. Her Holocaust-surviving parents had been denied entry into Israel by the British, who were in control of the land at that time. But guess what? The Brits left, and we came.

The State of Israel exists by the all-powerful hand of God. "'I will put My Spirit in you, and you shall live, and I will place you in your own land. Then you shall know that I, the LORD, have spoken it and performed it,' says the LORD" (Ezekiel 37:14). I will never apologize for living in the land of Israel. We are not there because we worked hard for it or paid for it. We are there because God put us there. Bringing Israel back to the land is His way of saying to the world, "Hey, look, it's Me. I am doing something amazing here. Better get ready for what comes next!"

But don't think that just because God brought us back to the land that it will all be babka and baklava. Israel is about to go through the most difficult period in their history. What we've experienced thus far will pale in comparison:

> At that time Michael shall stand up,
> the great prince who stands watch over the
>   sons of your people;
> and there shall be a time of trouble,
> such as never was since there was a nation,
> even to that time.
> And at that time your people shall be delivered,
> every one who is found written in the book
>   (Daniel 12:1).

These words are chilling to anyone who even understands a fraction of what took place in the Holocaust. Nothing in the past, including in 1930s and 1940s Europe, will be able to compare to the severity of what is to come. Yet, in the same way we read earlier that "he [Israel] shall be saved out of it [Jacob's trouble]" (Jeremiah 30:7), here in Daniel, we see that "at that time your people shall be delivered." Does that mean that God is going to give a blanket salvation to all of Israel? Absolutely not. Deliverance will come only to those who are "found written in the book." What book? The Lamb's book of life. And there is only one way to have your name written there: "God so loved the world that He gave His only begotten Son, that whoever believes in Him should not perish but have everlasting life" (John 3:16).

It is through faith in Yeshua the Messiah, Jesus Christ, that we receive salvation and our names are written in the Lamb's book of life. If your name is there, you have eternal life. If it is not, then you don't. It is a black-and-white proposition with absolutely no room for gray. So, when all Israel is saved, it is because the people will all call on the name of the true Messiah, Jesus Christ. But because this revival will take place at the end of the tribulation, not all Jews who are alive at the beginning of the seven years will find salvation. God said through Zechariah:

> "It shall come to pass in all the land,"
> says the LORD,
> "that two-thirds in it shall be cut off and die,
> but one-third shall be left in it:
> I will bring the one-third through the fire,
> will refine them as silver is refined,
> and test them as gold is tested.
> They will call on My name,
> and I will answer them.
> I will say, 'This is My people';
> and each one will say, 'The LORD is my God'"
> (Zechariah 13:8-9).

The current population of Israel is over nine million people. That means that six million Jews will not see the end of the tribulation. Today, as I look at my country, I see a nation that, to a large extent, has turned its back on God. It's very religious, but it is filled with people who honor God with their lips while their hearts are far from Him. I have no doubt that when the antichrist comes, the people of

Tel Aviv and many other Israeli cities will warmly embrace him. Many will happily choose to receive the mark of the beast. This is because, as Paul wrote, a "blindness in part has happened to Israel" (Romans 11:25). The tribulation will prepare their eyes to be opened, so that when Jesus returns, they will look at Him whom they have pierced and they will mourn as a sign of their repentance. It is this repentance that leads to a forgiveness that brings salvation.

THE ENEMY AND ISRAEL

Do you ever turn on the television, flip through the channels, and wonder, *How can people watch this stuff? Am I really this out of touch with the world?* If you are a believer, then, yes, you really are that out of touch with the world. At least you should be. This is because the world follows its master, the devil, and believers should follow their Master, God. And ever since the fall of mankind, whatever God hates the devil loves, and whatever God loves the devil hates. Nowhere is this more evident than in Satan's passionate hatred for the Jews, God's chosen people.

Throughout Israel's history, the devil has been trying to eliminate the nation. In ancient Egypt, when the Hebrew population was getting too big, Pharaoh got nervous and took decisive action. He said to the midwives, "When you do the duties of a midwife for the Hebrew women, and see them on the birthstools, if it is a son, then you shall kill him; but if it is a daughter, then she shall live" (Exodus 1:16). The midwives gave Pharaoh a thumbs up and a "Sure thing," then promptly ignored his order. This was the first attempted genocide of the Jewish people.

Fast-forward to the Persian exile. An official of King Ahasuerus named Haman became very upset when a man named Mordecai refused to pay him the respect that he thought he deserved. Upon hearing that Mordecai was a Jew, Haman decided to seek his revenge not just upon the man but upon his entire people group.

When Haman saw that Mordecai did not bow or pay him homage, Haman was filled with wrath. But he disdained to lay hands on Mordecai alone, for they had told him of the people of Mordecai. Instead, Haman sought to destroy all the Jews who were throughout the whole kingdom of Ahasuerus—the people of Mordecai (Esther 3:5-6).

As always, God was watching over His people and had already placed their savior in position. Queen Esther risked her life to let the king know of the plan. The king intervened, the Jews were saved, and Haman became the textbook definition of someone who is hoisted with one's own petard.

If there is one quality with which we can credit Satan, it is tenacity. He has had failure after failure when it comes to wiping out the Jews, but he still hasn't given up. Purges and pogroms have boiled up throughout the centuries, seeking localized genocide. Both Hitler and Stalin took their shot at killing off the Jewish people—Hitler with gas, Stalin with bullets. They're both dead now, but we Jews are still here. Not because we are strong and powerful, but because we have Someone who is strong and powerful watching over us. "For thus says the LORD of hosts: 'He sent Me after glory, to the nations which plunder you; for he who touches you touches the apple of His eye'" (Zechariah 2:8).

I've spent time in the Rocky Mountains of Colorado. When hiking, I was warned that if I saw a baby bear, I shouldn't approach it no matter how cute it might be. In fact, the best option is to get out of there as quickly as your feet will take you. Because where there is a baby bear, mama bear is nearby. If mama bear thinks you have any interest at all in her little cub, then it just might be game over for you.

Nations and empires have attacked God's people, and He has gone full mama bear back on them. Egypt was decimated by the Babylonian Empire and has never recovered. The Assyrian Empire is gone.

The Babylonian Empire is gone. The Roman Empire is gone. The Third Reich and the Soviet Union are gone.

But now the devil, in his scheming, has taken a new tact. If you can't take down Israel from the outside, then do it from within. As it stands now, no one can accuse Israel of being a godly nation. One stroll through Tel Aviv during Pride Month will tell you that we left the Mosaic law dead and buried far back in our history. And it is getting worse. In March 2021, Israel voted in such a way as to allow a progressive, liberal, post-Zionist "government of change" into office. That government lasted only one devastatingly bad year before it collapsed.

At the time of the Israeli prime minister's fall, many were celebrating. I was not. I knew that when the enemy attacked, he did not go after the government; he went after the people. It was not the Israeli government that had changed; it was the Israelis themselves. The country's left remains left. But the right has taken a major shift in the liberal direction. The enemy has breached the conservative fortress. Even Orthodox Jews in the Knesset were willing to partner with the Muslim Brotherhood and pro-LGBT parties just so they could kick Benjamin Netanyahu out of the prime minister's office. And despite Netanyahu now being voted back in, the previous government still acts as a bellwether indicating the direction the Israeli culture is moving. There are no standards anymore. There are no principles. The Jews are on a clear path toward progressive liberalism that will reach its peak with their acceptance of the antichrist. Once that happens, Satan will believe that he finally has them right where he wants them, primed for elimination.

But a heavenly sign in the book of Revelation tells us that, once again, it will not turn out quite as the devil has planned:

> Another sign appeared in heaven: behold, a great, fiery red dragon having seven heads and ten horns, and seven diadems on his heads. His tail drew a third of the stars

of heaven and threw them to the earth. And the dragon stood before the woman who was ready to give birth, to devour her Child as soon as it was born. She bore a male Child who was to rule all nations with a rod of iron. And her Child was caught up to God and His throne. Then the woman fled into the wilderness, where she has a place prepared by God, that they should feed her there one thousand two hundred and sixty days (Revelation 12:3-6).

The woman is Israel, the child is Jesus, and the dragon is the devil. When Jesus was born, Satan sought to kill Him right away, leading to King Herod's tragic order to "put to death all the male children who were in Bethlehem and in all its districts, from two years old and under" (Matthew 2:16). Jesus survived, carried out His work, and, when He was done with His earthly ministry, He was taken back up to His Father. That is why Stephen, just before being stoned to death, could say, "Look! I see the heavens opened and the Son of Man standing at the right hand of God!" (Acts 7:56).

The timeline of the Revelation 12 sign then rockets into the future. To escape the horrors of Satan's antichrist, the woman, who is Israel, will flee into the wilderness. Despite this being the time of Jacob's trouble, God still has compassion on His chosen people. He will prepare a place for them to hide out for 1,260 days, or three-and-a-half years. You see, even in the future, as the devil seeks to completely wipe out Israel, God will say, "Satan, you can go this far, but no further." The enemy has no choice except to obey. As much as he tries, Satan will never be able to destroy that which God loves.

THE WORLD AND ISRAEL

People are fascinated with that which is different. You go to an art gallery, and one of the displays has ten balls lined up—nine of them white and one of them blue—where will your eyes be drawn?

To the blue one, of course. Who cares about the white ones? They're the norm. But what's up with that blue one? Why is it there? Is there anything else that makes it different than just the color? What is the artist trying to say? And, seriously, how can they call this art?

The world has always had a fascination with the Jews. Why? Because we're different. We're the blue ball in the line of white-ball nations. From the beginning, our beliefs have been different, our lifestyles have been different, our traditions have been different. On top of that, we pride ourselves on being different. And not just different, but separate.

When King Balak hired the prophet Balaam to pronounce a curse over Israel, his plan backfired, and the prophet instead blessed the nation numerous times. In his first blessing, Balaam said,

> How shall I curse whom God has not cursed?
> And how shall I denounce whom the LORD has not denounced?
> For from the top of the rocks I see him,
> and from the hills I behold him;
> There! A people dwelling alone,
> not reckoning itself among the nations
> (Numbers 23:8-9).

What was true then has been true for most of Jewish history. We are a people dwelling alone. However, now, as the world recently saw with Israel's "government of change," we Jews are desperate to be "reckoned among the nations." Forget our history, forget our traditions, forget our calling. We don't want to dwell alone anymore. We want to be part of the gang!

How is the world responding? Now that we've painted ourselves so that we look just like all the other balls in the art display, the world is starting to open their arms to us. Our list of friends is expanding into Asia, Africa, Europe, South America, and, most surprisingly, the Middle East and North African Muslim countries.

No longer are we the guy at the party who condemningly glares as he sips his Diet Coke while everyone else is getting drunk. Now Israel is out slamming beers with everyone else. Our distinction is fading to the world.

Nothing has changed, however, in God's eyes. Israel continues to be the rebellious prodigal who wants nothing to do with Dad anymore. The method of rebellion may change over time, but the rejection of the Messiah does not. The Lord, however, continues in His role of Father, loving His child, grieving His child's decisions, and preparing for the moment when it will be time for tough-love parental discipline to get His kid back under control.

While Israel's relationship with much of the world is certainly improving, it will never be fully normalized. In 1982, the Steven Spielberg film *Poltergeist* was released. As is evident by the title, it is a ghost story that centers on the Freeling family, who have just moved into their new home in a beautiful, recently built housing development in California. Paranormal events begin taking place, and they soon take on a sinister air. Eventually, little Carole Anne Freeling mysteriously disappears into the house and all sorts of havoc takes place. Why is all this happening? It turns out that the new housing development was built on an ancient burial ground. So, while it looked beautiful above ground, below it was filled with death.

This is similar to what is happening with Israel's new friendships. Everything looks rosy on the surface, but below ground is a darkness that takes the form of continued rampant antisemitism around the world. In April 2021, the Anti-Defamation League (ADL) issued a press release titled "U.S. Antisemitic Incidents Remained at Historic High in 2020," in which they reported 2,024 incidents, the third highest total on record.[9] It's not just in America that the hatred of Jews still burns bright. In Europe, Jews continue to be harassed, assaulted, and have their synagogues burned. "The fight against this sickness [antisemitism] has become hopeless," wrote Brigette Wielheesen, a journalist and counterterrorism expert from the Netherlands. "If Jews are Europe's canary in the coal mine, that bird is no longer alive."[10]

Widespread antisemitism is not surprising, because people follow their master. They love what their master loves and they hate what their master hates. Satan hates the Jews. Therefore, he will do all he can to sustain antisemitism throughout the world, It is this hatred that he will use in his final attempt to wipe out the chosen people. Under the leadership of the antichrist, the nations will rise up against the Jewish people, and the nations will once again lose. Then they will be judged for their actions.

The prophet Joel wrote what God had to say about this future judgment:

> Behold, in those days and at that time,
> when I bring back the captives of Judah and Jerusalem,
> I will also gather all nations,
> and bring them down to the Valley of Jehoshaphat;
> and I will enter into judgment with them there
> on account of My people, My heritage Israel,
> whom they have scattered among the nations;
> they have also divided up My land (3:1-2).

This is essentially the Old Testament version of the sheep and the goats judgment. While on the Mount of Olives, Jesus taught His disciples, telling them of a future judgment in which He will separate the righteous from the unrighteous. To the righteous, He will say,

> Come, you blessed of My Father, inherit the kingdom
> prepared for you from the foundation of the world: for
> I was hungry and you gave Me food; I was thirsty and
> you gave Me drink; I was a stranger and you took Me
> in; I was naked and you clothed Me; I was sick and you

visited Me; I was in prison and you came to Me (Matthew 25:34-36).

Confused, the righteous will protest, saying, "Lord, as much as we'd like to take credit for those things, we can't remember ever doing that for You." The King will reply, "Assuredly, I say to you, inasmuch as you did it to one of the least of these My brethren, you did it to Me" (v. 40). In other words, if you treated well the brethren of Jesus, then you are a sheep. If you didn't, then you're a goat. In the Valley of Jehoshaphat, the criteria will be how the nations treated Israel. "I will enter judgment with them there on account of My people, My heritage Israel," the Lord says. During the tribulation, unbelievers will suffer unimaginably, but this will be a just punishment based on their rebellion against God and their persecution of the nation that He loves and that He chose for Himself.

THE CHURCH AND ISRAEL

If the world hates what God loves, the church should do exactly the opposite. How can believers call themselves followers of God if they don't passionately love that which God loves? Yet so many Christians want nothing to do with Israel. "Modern Israel is not the real Israel," they say. "How can a nation that is so secular with such a small evangelical Christian population possibly be the chosen people of God?" If sin and rebellion were the standards a father used to disown his child, I'm guessing that many of you reading this book would be parentless right now. Is that really how our God, who is the perfect expression of love (1 John 4:8), would treat those He called to be His own? If so, those of us believers who are trusting in the perfect love of God for our eternal life probably ought to be a little nervous right now that our own sins don't cross that mysterious expulsion line.

Also, if Israel no longer exists, what do you do with all those Israel-centered prophecies that are yet to be fulfilled? Oh, I see the hands of all my Replacement Theology readers just shot up. "The plan was always for the church to be the true Israel," you say. "The nation was just there in the beginning to get the ball rolling. So, when Israel magnificently tanked their mission, the church was ready to take over. Since then, the church has carried on the mission of being God's light in the darkness in perfect love and righteousness. Well, maybe not quite perfect, but at least a whole lot better than those Jews."

I've had believers in Replacement Theology say to me, "The belief that the church replaced Israel has its roots in the early church. It has been around since Origen and Augustine in the third and fourth centuries." I tell them, "I can do you one better. Replacement Theology has been around since the first century—which is why Paul had to write Romans 11 to counter it!"

> I say then, has God cast away His people? Certainly not! (v. 1).

> What does the divine response say to him? "I have reserved for Myself seven thousand men who have not bowed the knee to Baal." Even so then, at this present time there is a remnant according to the election of grace (vv. 4-5).

> I say then, have they stumbled that they should fall? Certainly not! (v. 11).

> If their being cast away is the reconciling of the world, what will their acceptance be but life from the dead? (v. 15).

> I do not desire, brethren, that you should be ignorant of this mystery, lest you should be wise in your own opinion, that blindness in part has happened to Israel until the fullness of the Gentiles has come in. And so all Israel will be saved (vv. 25-26).

> Concerning the gospel they are enemies for your sake, but concerning the election they are beloved for the sake

of the fathers. For the gifts and the calling of God are irrevocable (vv. 28-29).

God has committed them all to disobedience, that He might have mercy on all (v. 32).

Time and again in Romans 11, Paul assures the reader that God still loves Israel and has a plan for them. Twice he gives the emphatic, "Certainly not!" Throughout, he speaks in temporal terms—this is the situation now, but this is what will be in the future. He writes of a remnant. When has God ever removed a righteous remnant from His presence because of the sins of the wicked? Then there is that word "irrevocable." Such a powerful, no-caveat, no-wiggle-room expression. God called His people into an irrevocable promise through Abraham, so quit trying to conjure up doctrinal twists so you can revoke it! Yes, it is true that the church is made up of the spiritual descendants of Abraham. It consists of those who "believed God, and it was credited to [them] as righteousness" (see Romans 4:3). Amen! Praise the Lord! That is where my hope is as a physical and spiritual member of Abraham.

But just because there is a church made up of the spiritual descendants of Abraham, why must you now say that physical ancestry from Abraham means nothing? Read the Abrahamic covenant again:

Get out of your country,
from your family
and from your father's house,
to a land that I will show you.
I will make you a great nation;
I will bless you
and make your name great;
and you shall be a blessing.

I will bless those who bless you,
and I will curse him who curses you;
and in you all the families of the earth shall be blessed
(Genesis 12:1-3).

Why do you feel compelled to allegorize or spiritualize this? The
land is not promised to the church, but to Abraham's physical descendants. I agree that the church is a great spiritual nation made up of
those chosen by God, as Peter makes perfectly clear:

You are a chosen generation, a royal priesthood, a holy
nation, His own special people, that you may proclaim
the praises of Him who called you out of darkness into
His marvelous light; who once were not a people but are
now the people of God, who had not obtained mercy but
now have obtained mercy (1 Peter 2:9-10).

However, that has nothing to do with the physical lineage of Abraham, who are also clearly chosen by God:

You, Israel, are My servant,
Jacob whom I have chosen,
the descendants of Abraham My friend.
You whom I have taken from the ends of the earth,
and called from its farthest regions,
and said to you,
"You are My servant,
I have chosen you and have not cast you away"
(Isaiah 41:8-9).

Since Abraham was first called out of Ur, the people of Israel have
belonged to God. He loved them, and He loves them still. He wanted

a relationship with them, and He wants it still. This is the foundational purpose for the tribulation. God loves the people of Israel, and He wants them back. But He wants them to *want* to come back. At the end of the seven years of the tribulation, they will do just that.

A QUESTION
OF OVERKILL

It has been a hectic morning for Daniel. The kids seemed determined not to make it to school on time, which put his wife in a foul mood. By the time he pulled out of the driveway, both he and the love of his life had said things they regretted, and both of his children had said things that he was going to make sure they regretted when he got home tonight. The carpool line at the school seemed especially long today, and by the time he drove by his favorite coffee shop, he knew there was no time to stop to pick up his usual muffin and dosage of caffeine.

After arriving at the office where Daniel was a mid-level IT guy, his stomach was growling, and he knew that it would be a long slog to lunchtime. As he passed the break room on the way to his desk, he saw a small box on a counter. Salvation! It was a snack box put there by a local charity. The staff could choose the treat they wanted. Then, using the honor system, pay the suggested donation by dropping money into a built-in slot.

Reaching into his back pocket, Daniel was confronted with the realization that in all the chaos that had taken place earlier, he had left his wallet at home. He checked his front pockets for any spare change. Nothing! "Unbelievable," he muttered, as he turned to walk away.

But then he stopped. Would anyone really notice one missing snack? Besides, he had made purchases from this box numerous times before, sometimes even putting in more than the suggested donation because the money was for charity. Casually looking around and seeing the coast was clear, he quickly snatched a package of pistachios, then placed his hand over the slot to mimic dropping money in. Hurriedly, he found his desk, turned on his computer, opened the package of nuts, and began working.

The hours passed and the busyness of his day soon put the pistachio caper out of his mind. Then he received a memo that his supervisor wanted to see him. That was never good. A sense of foreboding caused him to walk a little slower toward his destination. When he stepped into the office, his fears were realized when he found not just his supervisor, but the head of the HR department, the CFO, and the CEO of the company waiting for him.

Daniel remained standing while the others silently sat, glaring at him. A monitor blinked to life and a video played of him scanning the break room, grabbing a pack of pistachios, then placing his obviously empty hand over the money slot.

"I've never seen anything so disgusting in my life," said his supervisor. "Stealing from a charity. Daniel, you're fired."

Stunned, Daniel looked from face to face for some sign that this was a big joke, but the others looked stern as ever.

"It was just a bag of pistachios!"

A sound came from the door behind him, and two police officers walked in. They threw Daniel against the wall and searched him. Then they handcuffed him, and a quick drive later, he was booked into jail. The next three months of arraignment, depositions, and trial flew by, finally ending with a sentence of 15 to 25 years for theft, followed by the slam of the judge's gavel.

As Daniel was led away, he was heard to once again mutter, "But it was only a bag of pistachios!"

I believe that most of us would agree that the sentence given to Daniel was excessive. Yes, it was wrong to take the nuts. But firing, jail, and an extended sentence in the iron bar hotel? The time doesn't seem to fit the crime.

That's how many people view the tribulation. A reading of the seal judgments, followed by the trumpet judgments, followed by the bowl judgments, often leads Christians and non-Christians alike to say, "Really, God? Isn't that a touch of overkill?" This is especially true when we consider that the vast majority of the world's sinful population are not murderers and abusers. They're just snack-stealing sinners. Whatever happened to mercy?

On the flip side, we know that God is just. He will not punish those who do not deserve to be punished. He also will not penalize people beyond what their sins call for. But can you really tell me that the sweet old lady down the street who always bakes cookies for the children on the block, just because she hasn't received Jesus as her Savior and Lord, somehow merits the judgments that we read of in the book of Revelation? Honestly, many of the dear women and men that I know here in Israel would give you the shirts off their backs. Are they destined for wrath just because they follow a works religion in which they are trying to prove themselves to God? As much as it pains me, I must answer yes.

In the previous chapter, we saw that the tribulation is primarily about disciplining the Jews so that they will finally be brought to the point that they will look upon the One whom they have pierced and respond with mourning and repentance. However, there is also a punitive nature to the seven years of horror. The wider purpose of the tribulation includes bringing wrath upon the world as a just recompense for the sins of mankind. Eventually, following the millennial kingdom, all unredeemed humanity and all sin-tainted creation will come to an end. Then the Lord will start over with new heavens and a new earth, populated with those who chose to follow Him with their whole hearts.

Does spiritually dead mankind deserve the wrath of the tribulation? Sadly, the answer is yes. And the reason is sin. Adam inaugurated sin into humanity, and since then, we've practiced hard to develop our expertise. To understand the tribulation, we must understand sin. But rather than simply providing some clinical definition of sin, I want to begin by using the world around us as a living illustration of both the extreme nature of sin and how humanity has perfected its execution. Once we see sin's tragic effects, then we will go back and look at what sin really is.

SIN'S TRAGIC EFFECTS

The Moral State of the World

It is easy to read about Sodom and Gomorrah in Genesis 19 and think, *Wow! What depraved and messed-up cities!* But a perusal of cable television and the internet or a visit to a pride parade or a reading of the minutes of an annual convention of many mainline denominations might have you expecting a weather forecast of "Fiery, with a chance of brimstone."

What we are witnessing is the natural outworking of our internal sin nature. God saw the inclinations of our hearts and, rather than forcing us to obey Him, He allowed us to make our own choices.

> Therefore God also gave them up to uncleanness, in the lusts of their hearts, to dishonor their bodies among themselves, who exchanged the truth of God for the lie, and worshiped and served the creature rather than the Creator, who is blessed forever. Amen (Romans 1:24-25).

This world is in an ever-deteriorating moral spiral. We have sin down to an art form. Chances are Lot would look at us and say, "Thank heavens I only have to deal with these sick shmoes here in Sodom!" This constant decline in our morality stems from the fact that we follow our master, Satan, who is determined that this world be the exact opposite from what God created it to be. The prophet Isaiah condemned those with this contrary-to-holiness attitude, saying,

> Woe to those who call evil good, and good evil;
> who put darkness for light, and light for darkness;
> who put bitter for sweet, and sweet for bitter! (5:20).

Anything that the Bible describes as works of darkness is today being celebrated and paraded. On the other hand, those who want to carry out works of light, such as helping those who are confused about their gender identity or coming alongside women with unplanned pregnancies, must do so in secret. They must work underground, hiding their righteous activities. But this isn't the first time that the world has seen this reversal of ethical norms. In fact, in every empire and every civilization, we've seen the same cycle of moral deterioration that eventually leads to societal collapse.

Early nineteenth-century philosopher Georg Hegel wrote, "What experience and history teach us is this—that nations and governments have never learned anything from history, or acted on any lessons they may have drawn from it."[11] Governments not learning from past mistakes? I know that's hard to believe. Toward the end of the eighteenth century, historian Edward Gibbon wrote the monumental six-volume work *The Decline and Fall of the Roman Empire*, in which he described exactly what the title indicates. Yet with that example clearly laid out, America and Western Europe are still skipping arm in arm right down the same path to destruction.

This repetitive cycle of self-immolation happens because at some point in each society, the moral compass goes haywire. It's like a polar shift occurs and the needle just starts spinning. Eric Snow wrote in 2011, "The growth of wealth and comfort clearly can undermine the values of character, such as self-sacrifice and discipline, that led to a given empire's creation. Then the empire so affected by moral decline grows weaker and more vulnerable to destruction by forces arising inside or outside of it."[12] Early generations build up through selflessness. Later generations tear down through selfishness.

I can see this very transformation taking place in Israel. Born on a foundation of mutual sacrifice and a spirit of unity, Israel has been morphing into a spoiled, me-first nation. This was evident in the election of the "government of change" that was much less interested in the health of the nation than the comfort and emotional safety of the individual. And even though this weak, worthless administration has collapsed, I don't hold out hope for a reversal of direction. Like the transition from Joshua to the period of the Judges, the new generation didn't experience the miraculous hand of God during the early years of Israel's statehood. Thus, the current population of the nation has moved to the time of everyone doing "what was right in [their] own eyes" (Judges 17:6).

In a list of the primary indicators that lead to the decline of an empire, at least three are moral in nature. First, there is increased sexual immorality. And for those of you heterosexuals who immediately point your condemning finger at the LGBT community, please notice the four fingers that are pointing back at you. Those fingers are directed at the huge number of Christian couples who are living together outside of marriage. They are aimed at men who justify their pornography habits, women who can't wait for the next one in the series of their favorite sex-charged romance novels, and parents who bring crudity and softcore pornography into their homes through their cable boxes. Often, just the commercials during sporting events are enough to chink away at the innocence of our children. Sexual immorality is the ultimate act of "me first," and "me first" is the most destructive attitude in a society.

Second is the undermining of the family structure. Starting with the very first couple on the face of the earth, God established family. "Therefore a man shall leave his father and mother and be joined to his wife, and they shall become one flesh" (Genesis 2:24). Once again, because this is something God cherishes, the enemy does all he can to destroy it. The marriage vow "Till death do us part" is no longer taken seriously. The definition of a family has become whatever someone wants it to be. And, most horrific of all, the killing of a baby in its mother's womb is considered nothing but a routine medical procedure. I'm sick to death of hearing about pro-choice. The opposite of pro-life is pro-death, at least the last time I studied English.

A third morality-related indicator of the decline of an empire is a lack of personal responsibility. Fatherless homes, me-based social values, snowflake-centric societal rules, and an overwhelming dependence upon the government for provision and protection have transformed much of the Western world into soft-willed simps who are continuously looking for someone to blame for any word or action that makes them feel offended or less than safe. Hurt feelings quickly turn into accusations, internet shaming, canceling, protests, riots, political malfeasance, abuse by the justice system, and, in a growing number of cases in Europe, incarceration. Because truth can be deemed hurtful and offensive, it is being canceled along with its purveyors. And without a foundation of truth, there is nothing left to hold up a society.

All the boxes for a collapsing empire are being checked right now by countless nations in the West and beyond. And we should not be surprised. Paul already told us in Romans what was coming:

> Therefore God also gave them up to uncleanness, in the lusts of their hearts, to dishonor their bodies among themselves, who exchanged the truth of God for the lie, and worshiped and served the creature rather than the Creator, who is blessed forever. Amen.

> For this reason God gave them up to vile passions. For even their women exchanged the natural use for what is

against nature. Likewise also the men, leaving the natural use of the woman, burned in their lust for one another, men with men committing what is shameful, and receiving in themselves the penalty of their error which was due.

And even as they did not like to retain God in their knowledge, God gave them over to a debased mind, to do those things which are not fitting; being filled with all unrighteousness, sexual immorality, wickedness, covetousness, maliciousness; full of envy, murder, strife, deceit, evil-mindedness; *they are* whisperers, backbiters, haters of God, violent, proud, boasters, inventors of evil things, disobedient to parents, undiscerning, untrustworthy, unloving, unforgiving, unmerciful; who, knowing the righteous judgment of God, that those who practice such things are deserving of death, not only do the same but also approve of those who practice them (1:24-32).

How often do we in the church accusingly stop at the second paragraph of that passage without moving to the minefield of sins in the third paragraph—many of them of the more "acceptable" variety of offenses amongst the Christian crowd? What Paul warned was happening to the Roman Empire is now taking place in the Western empire. We would be fools to think that it will end any differently for us.

The Geopolitical State of the World

From 2016–2020, I used to wake up every morning and pinch myself, thinking, *Could it get any better than this?* And then one day, I woke up, looked at the headlines, and pulled the covers back over my head. In November 2020, the US held elections that were, well, not quite kosher. Then, in March 2021, my country, Israel, also held a vote. The results were essentially the same in both. Two "governments of change" came into power.

In the US, the primary goal was to be everything the previous administration was not, and to find ways to make everyone associated with the former holder of the top office pay for their "treachery," both financially and with their freedom. In Israel, the vindictiveness of the new power structure was primarily directed at the former prime minister. And in both nations, the governmental focus changed from national strength and economic soundness to social change and personal and environmental protection.

Seeing an opening, many of the bad actors of the world who had been held at bay by the strong leadership of the previous administrations now saw an opportunity. As I write this, Russia is still on its destructive path pushing through Ukraine. North Korea is testing hypersonic missiles and testing nuclear devices. Iran has all the materials it needs to create a nuclear weapon and is just waiting for the decision to go ahead with its manufacturing. China has Taiwan surrounded with regular "patrols" and is daily violating the island nation's sovereignty in the air and on the water.

If you have been waiting for a time of "wars and rumors of wars" ever since you first read Matthew 24:6, your wait is over. Just come to the Middle East. Iraq and Syria are rife with Iran-backed Shiite terrorist militias. The Lebanese government has become a puppet of the terrorist group Hezbollah. The Houthi rebels in Yemen are constantly finding targets to blow up in their own country and next door in Saudi Arabia. Overseeing all this mayhem is the evil Islamist regime in Tehran, which is in a continuous game of live-fire chess with Israel. A very short distance from my house is the Ramat David Airbase of the Israeli Air Force, which is home to three F-16 squadrons. Many are the times that I see fighter jets take off fully loaded with armaments and return with the underside of their wings empty.

It took only one generation for the sin of Adam and Eve to result in one man taking another's life. This is not surprising. As we've seen, Satan hates everything that God loves. God created life to be held up as sacred, and He commanded humanity to honor it and protect it. It is no wonder that the enemy had the destruction of life at the top of his to-do list. The battles between nations and within nations are simply a continuation of the sinful pattern that he began thousands of years ago when he tempted one sibling to kill another on the wrong side of the gates to paradise.

The Physical State of the World

Sin is a destroyer. If you want evidence of this, simply look at the deterioration of the natural world. Our planet started with six days of "and it was good," which was epitomized in a lush, rich oasis of beauty called Eden.

> The LORD God planted a garden eastward in Eden, and there He put the man whom He had formed. And out of the ground the LORD God made every tree grow that is pleasant to the sight and good for food. The tree of life was also in the midst of the garden, and the tree of the knowledge of good and evil (Genesis 2:8-9).

All was perfect inside and outside of the garden. Then what happened? Deception, rebellion, and punishment. When Adam sinned, the perfection of creation was tainted. Paul stated it very succinctly: "The wages of sin is death" (Romans 6:23). Death entered the body of Adam, leading to the mortality of all humanity. Death entered the soul of Adam, separating him and all his descendants from a holy God. And death entered the natural world, beginning a gradual corrosion of the earth's perfection. The penalty given to Adam includes God's declaration, "Cursed is the ground for your sake" (Genesis 3:17). The evidence that God takes His own words seriously is all around us.

With death came disease. The COVID pandemic was an experience new to this generation, but it certainly wasn't new to mankind. In the mid-fourteenth century, the bubonic plague, or Black Death, horrifically stole the lives of 25-30 million in Europe alone. In the early twentieth century, the Spanish flu killed an estimated 20 to 50 million people. Pestilence and disease were not part of the "it was good" of God's creation. It is sin that opened the door to the Asian flu, the Hong Kong flu, AIDS, SARS, MERS, Swine flu, Ebola, Zika, and all other sicknesses.

With death came natural disasters. Earthquakes, tsunamis, volcanoes, and famines were also not a part of God's creation. There was no tornado shelter in Eden. Adam didn't have to teach Eve to stand in the doorway when the ground began to shake. Once imperfection entered into God's perfect creation, an expiration date was stamped on the heavens and the earth. Now they are rotting year after year, and will continue to do so until God creates a new heavens and new earth. That re-creation is a day that Paul said all created things long for, when "creation itself also will be delivered from the bondage of corruption into the glorious liberty of the children of God" (Romans 8:21).

Because most of humanity lives as if all that matters is the natural world, the deterioration of that world causes great fear. In the past, civilizations made gods out of the sun, the moon, rainclouds, and other elements of nature they didn't understand. If you are afraid of something and you are powerless to control it, then the best option is to appease it through worship and sacrifice. The same is true today with the purveyors of the climate change religion. In 2006, while promoting his movie, global warming high priest Al Gore predicted that unless drastic changes were made in ten years, the world would pass the point of no return. This time frame is one that his loyal acolytes at the UN have been touting since 1989. The decade passed, and the fact that I am currently typing this sentence on my computer is evidence that the world is still here.

I do agree with climate pastor Gore in two areas. First, we should take care of our environment. While I wouldn't go to the extremes to which he and other members of the climate cult go, we are to be good stewards of God's creation. We should respect it and do our best to keep it clean and safe. Second, I agree that if we continue on our present path, the world is doomed. However, if we change our path and do everything the Church of Gore wants, the world is still doomed. That's because its destruction is not based on anything today's humanity is doing. The planet will meet its end because of what the first man did all those years ago. That is the power of sin.

The Spiritual State of the World

It is the spiritually dead nature of the world that has caused the moral, geopolitical, and physical states of the world to be such as they are. In their clandestine meeting, Jesus told the Pharisee Nicodemus, "This is the condemnation, that the light has come into the world, and men loved darkness rather than light, because their deeds were evil. For everyone practicing evil hates the light and does not come to the light, lest his deeds should be exposed" (John 3:19-20). Humanity hates the light because their deeds are evil. What do we call those evil deeds? Sin.

This is a cringy illustration, and I'm going to apologize for it even before I write it. Humanity's comfort living with their sins is like a toddler wetting its diaper, then not wanting it to be changed because it feels warm and comforting. I'm the father of four kids, three of them boys. I know wet diapers. And as a parent, I also know that an unchanged diaper can cause all sorts of problems like odors, rashes, and infections. But all the child cares about is "Hmmm, this kinda feels good." They have no thought for the consequences.

That is the state of our sin-soaked culture. Sadly, the place that used to tell people to get their diapers changed cannot be counted on to do so anymore. God ordained the church to be His spokespeople to tell those who have become comfortable with their sins that they have a problem that must be taken care of. If they don't deal with the issue, serious ramifications will come both in this life and in the next. However, too many churches have given up that responsibility. From the pulpits, pastors are telling their people, "If that warm, squishy feeling makes you feel good, then that's just great. God doesn't care if your diaper is wet or dry, as long as you are happy and you are living your best life now." Meanwhile, the skin is turning red, the rash is spreading, the sores are breaking out, and the infection has begun.

Thankfully for all of us, I am now going to leave that illustration behind. This doctrine of "God doesn't care about sin; He just wants you to be happy" is spreading like wildfire through the church. I have a friend in southeast Asia who now teaches that all people are saved. It doesn't matter what you believe or how you live. Not surprisingly, the celebrities in that country love to hear him teach because he is giving them free license to live as they please with no eternal consequences.

Back to Jesus' encounter with Nicodemus. He went on to say, "But he who does the truth comes to the light, that his deeds may be clearly seen, that they have been done in God" (John 3:21). It's interesting how when you see the light, when you truly come to faith in Jesus Christ, then you want that purifying Sonlight to rid you of all that was dragging you down and making you feel filthy. And when He does, it is a feeling like none other. It's better than a cleansing shower after a hard day of work.

Being clean will make us feel great, but it will also make us stand out from everyone else. One look at our stainless clothes and our freshly scrubbed bodies, and the unrepentant masses will become acutely aware of the dirt and grime that is covering them. In the upper room, Jesus told His disciples, "If the world hates you, you know that it hated Me before it hated you. If you were of the world, the world would love its own. Yet because you are not of the world, but I chose you out of the world, therefore the world hates you" (John 15:18-19). If you are a Christian and the world loves you, then something must be wrong with the way you are living.

Don't get me wrong; it should not be our goal to get people to hate us. We are called to sacrificially love those around us, to do all we can to lead them to the Messiah. The hatred will come from their side because of the sin-sick state of their souls. The light of Christ in us illuminates the darkness of their deeds, and that is an untenable happening in our culture of "It's all good as long as it makes you happy." Our mission is to hug the porcupines, recognizing that we will likely pay a price. Yet the pain will be worth it just to witness the joy and freedom that results from a forgiven life and a heavenly eternity for someone who was dead in their sins.

WHAT IS SIN?

Now that we've seen the tragic effects of sin on all of creation, it's time to define what sin really is. There have been books written about this subject, and a simple Google search will offer you lengthy technical expositions nuancing the very concept. And if that is what you love to read, fantastic! Have at it. My goal in my writing, however, is to take difficult concepts and make them easy to understand. So, I will give you this concise definition: Sin is willful rebellion against God. The Lord spoke of such defiance through the prophet Isaiah:

> I have stretched out My hands all day long to a
> rebellious people,
> who walk in a way that is not good,
> according to their own thoughts;
> a people who provoke Me to anger continually to
> My face (65:2-3).

First, notice that the people were acting according to their own thoughts. What a perfect description of today's morality. When it comes to our behavior, God has outlined very clearly what is acceptable and what is unacceptable. Throughout the New Testament, you will find lists of sins such as the one in Galatians, which prohibits "adultery, fornication, uncleanness, lewdness, idolatry, sorcery, hatred, contentions, jealousies, outbursts of wrath, selfish ambitions, dissensions, heresies, envy, murders, drunkenness, revelries, and the like" (5:19-21), and Jesus' list in the Gospel of Mark, which includes "evil thoughts, adulteries, fornications, murders, thefts, covetousness, wickedness, deceit, lewdness, an evil eye, blasphemy, pride, foolishness" (7:21-22).

These lists represent God's thoughts about what is right and wrong, and because of His perfect holiness and righteousness, we can be assured that His thoughts are correct. When we reject God's dictates about behavior, we are saying to Him, in a horrible twisting of Scripture, "Sorry, Lord, but as the heavens are higher than the earth, so are my ways higher than Your ways, and my thoughts than Your thoughts." God says, "Do not do this." We respond, "Okay, I won't do it…at least not too often."

That is rebellion. Imagine giving a set of house rules to your children and hearing them respond with, "Cute list, Mom. Now let us tell you how it's going to be." That is what sin is. It is saying, "Lord, I want to carry out this act or think this thought or indulge this lust more than I want to be obedient to You." How should God respond to that? Should the almighty Creator simply shrug and say, "Well, as long as you're having a good time"?

But sin is even more heinous than simple rebellion. It is wanton rebellion. The second characteristic identified in the Isaiah passage was that Judah's defiance was to God's face. Sin is making an obscene gesture to the Lord as you commit your lawbreaking. Now, you may shrink back and say, "I would never do that to anyone, let alone God." But that is exactly what we are doing when we ignore that little moment of Holy Spirit conviction that tells us to stop, and instead, we push through to carry out our sin. It is saying, in that moment, "Despite all that You have done for me and all that You have promised me, Lord, I love me more than I love You. So, I'm going ahead with it." Sin is willful, in-Your-face-God disobedience.

Unbelievers don't have that same Spirit conviction, but they are nevertheless responsible for their actions. Paul makes it clear that Holy Spirit or not, people know when they are doing wrong. Everyone has "the work of the law written in their hearts, their conscience also bearing witness, and between themselves their thoughts accusing or else excusing them" (Romans 2:15). Every sin is a deliberate, malicious act of rebellion by the creation against its Creator. And the idea that God's love will just overlook sin is an affront against His perfection.

The tribulation will be more terrible than you could ever imagine. But is it too much? Is it overkill? Sadly, it is not. It is the just punishment for every person who has sinned, a list that includes the name of everyone who has ever been born.

But there is hope. Returning to a passage we read earlier, we now complete the verse: "The wages of sin is death, but the gift of God is eternal life in Christ Jesus our Lord" (Romans 6:23).

Through our actions, those of us who are still alive at the time will have earned our ticket to the tribulation, and all will warrant the subsequent eternity apart from God. But in a selfless act of sacrifice, Jesus took that deserved penalty upon Himself and paid our price. He offers us freedom from our punishment as a gift, absolutely free of charge. All He asks is that we believe He is who He said He is, and that we receive Him as our Lord and Savior. Could it really be that simple? Paul says, "Absolutely!"

> If you confess with your mouth the Lord Jesus and believe in your heart that God has raised Him from the dead, you will be saved. For with the heart one believes unto righteousness, and with the mouth confession is made unto salvation (Romans 10:9-10).

If you are afraid of the coming tribulation, let the Messiah remove that fear. Repent of your sins, turn to Jesus, and receive Him into your life. Let today be the day of your salvation!

ORDER AND MERCY

I will admit that the last chapter was difficult to write. It was necessarily pessimistic because there is no upside to sin. The momentary pleasure we receive from going against God's standard is like buying a brand new sports car with a high-interest car loan while working a minimum-wage job. You'll feel great as you drive the car off the lot, go racing up and down the streets, and show it off to your friends—all the way until you receive that first monthly statement. Then you will be forced to confront face to face the long-term ramifications of the stupid choice you just made.

All have sinned. Therefore, all humanity is deserving of punishment, and the ultimate punishment is eternal separation from God. That is the spiritual death that Paul said we each earn through our sins—our "wages." Jews deserve it because of their rebellious choices and their rejection of the Messiah. Gentiles deserve spiritual death for the very same reasons. Each person who has ever been born has bought the car, and now we are facing a debt that we can't pay. The penalty for our actions is just.

If you don't make the payments on the sports car, what will happen? The bank will come and repossess it. Fair enough. But what if the repo people came to your house, beat you up, burned down your home, then intentionally ran over you with the car as they drove off? Wouldn't that be a little excessive? Again, that's how some people view the tribulation. "Why doesn't God just kill everyone and then let them face judgment? Why must He torture them with the seals and trumpets and bowls first?" To some, this is akin to rather than just swatting a fly, capturing it, tearing off its wings, pulling off its legs, then letting it starve to death. Isn't the tribulation just torture for torture's sake?

It is true that we can see purpose in the horrors of the tribulation because they are what will bring Israel to repentance and salvation. But why must everyone else be dragged into this seven-year restoration process? Couldn't God have found an easier way? Are the Jews really so stubborn that it will take seven years of discipline before they finally learn their lesson? Couldn't a perfectly wise, all-knowing God have accomplished this in a much shorter time, and without bringing the rest of the world into it?

The answers to those last two questions are as follows: First, as a Jew, I can say that yes, we are really that stubborn. Second, again yes, God could have done it a different way. However, He couldn't have done it a better way. How do I know? Because this is the perfect plan of a perfect God. We've already seen in the previous chapters that He is a God of justice. What we see in this faultless plan of the tribulation is that He is also a God of order and, believe it or not, a God of mercy.

GOD OF ORDER

With God there is no randomness. There is no chaos. There are no worlds accidentally spinning off their axes, nor cells mutating in ways He didn't expect. To some, that may sound boring. Isn't it in the unpredictable that we find excitement, adventure, and even beauty? Good point, but even the seemingly random and unpredictable are bound within certain sets of rules. The joy of experiencing love at first sight while mundanely shopping for milk at a grocery store would take a less-than-idyllic turn if, at the same moment, gravity was turned off or you discovered you were suddenly aging backward.

Just like a child can safely carry out little pretend adventures knowing that a parent is controlling their environment, so can we live our lives with our little thrills and surprises knowing that God has surrounded us with His perfectly dependable systems. We rely upon the order of God because it is the framework from which we can learn and define the world around us. It is this faultless structure that also allows us to have hope for the future. The orderliness of God extends from the systems of creation to the design for our salvation to the blueprint He has laid out for the conclusion of this world and the beginning of the next. Thus, we know that the tribulation isn't just an option in God's end-times scenario; it is a necessity.

Order in Salvation—Two Births

The perfect order of God is seen throughout His plan for the redemption, restoration, and future glorification of humanity. First, we see it in the two births of the believer. Everyone is born at least once. If you were hatched, transported from another galaxy, or spontaneously generated from some primordial ooze, then I think you likely have bigger issues than can be dealt with in this book. When you were born, you were born a sinner. "But wait," you say. "It says right on my birth certificate that I am a Christian." I hate to burst your bubble, but your birth certificate is wrong. No one is born a Christian; in fact, the exact opposite is true:

> The LORD saw that the wickedness of man was great in the earth, and that every intent of the thoughts of his heart was only evil continually (Genesis 6:5).

According to King David, his continually evil heart was there right from the beginning:

> Behold, I was brought forth in iniquity,
> and in sin my mother conceived me (Psalm 51:5).

The spiritual revolt that started with Adam's bite took hold. It then spread like wildfire throughout humanity and exists to this very day:

> Through one man sin entered the world, and death through sin, and thus death spread to all men, because all sinned (Romans 5:12).

Because all have sinned, we can't just point a finger at Adam and blame it all on him. He may have poured water on the dirt, but we jumped in of our own accord and wallowed in the mud. God is a God of order, and sin is an act of disorder. Thus, it is no surprise that right from the beginning, knowing our propensity toward sin, He provided a means of washing the mud off our bodies so we could once again be clean.

> God so loved the world that He gave His only begotten Son, that whoever believes in Him should not perish but have everlasting life. For God did not send His Son into the world to condemn the world, but that the world through Him might be saved. He who believes in Him is not condemned; but he who does not believe is condemned already, because he has not believed in the name of the only begotten Son of God (John 3:16-18).

There are two categories of people in this world: the "not condemned" and the "condemned already." No one is born believing in Jesus. Therefore, we all begin in the latter category. Jesus said that to move from the condemned already to the not condemned, "You must be born again" (John 3:7). This is the second birth.

The phrase "born again" has become so popular within the culture that it is almost to the point of being cliché. Some even use it as a pejorative against Bible-believing Christians, not really understanding what the term means. To Nicodemus the Pharisee, being "born again" was simply crazy talk, sounding absurd biologically, and likely near blasphemous ethnically and theologically.

The esteemed teacher asked Jesus, "How can a man be born when he is old? Can he enter a second time into his mother's womb and be born?" (v. 4). This was a totally fair question asked by a man who was not mocking Jesus, but who was honestly seeking clarification for a weird-sounding statement. And Jesus gave him an honest, straightforward explanation, saying, "Most assuredly, I say to you, unless one is born of water and the Spirit, he cannot enter the kingdom of God. That which is born of the flesh is flesh, and that which is born of the Spirit is spirit" (vv. 5-6).

While Jesus' statement was biologically bizarre, there were ethnic and spiritual ramifications to His words. For the Jews, their relationship with God was based on who they were. They counted themselves as special because they were the descendants of Abraham. And they were right in believing that. But their exceptionalism was not salvific in nature. It was a uniqueness of ancestry. Now, here was Jesus saying, "Yeah, it's great you were born a Jew, but now you have to be born again into something better." You can almost hear Nicodemus's inner monologue crying out, *What? What's better than being born a Jew?* Jesus made it clear that it was not the first birth of the flesh that mattered; it's the second birth—of the spirit—that makes an eternal difference.

When Jesus was speaking to the Samaritan woman, He told her,

> Woman, believe Me, the hour is coming when you will neither on this mountain, nor in Jerusalem, worship the Father. You worship what you do not know; we know what

we worship, for salvation is of the Jews. But the hour is
coming, and now is, when the true worshipers will worship
the Father in spirit and truth; for the Father is seeking such
to worship Him. God is Spirit, and those who worship
Him must worship in spirit and truth (John 4:21-24).

"But, Amir, salvation is from God. How can you say that it's of
the Jews?" I didn't come up with that; I only read it. Those words
came from Jesus' mouth, and He said them knowing that He was
the Jew from whom salvation would come.

Sometimes people in the church forget that Jesus was not a Christian. He was never a follower of Christ. He didn't grow up going to
summer church camp, nor did He ever help pass out bulletins at a
crowded Christmas Eve service. He never even memorized one verse
out of the Gospels or the epistles. Remember who He was. Jesus was
100 percent a Jew, born in Bethlehem of Judea, of the tribe of Judah.
It was from that one Jew that salvation came to the world.

And now He was telling both Nicodemus and the Samaritan woman
that salvation isn't about who your ancestors were. Instead, it's about
who you are now. It isn't about the birth of water; it's about the birth
of the spirit. And when one's spirit is given life at their rebirth, it is
life evermore—everything in its perfect time and order.

Order in Consequences—Two Deaths

If there are two births, a physical and a spiritual birth, then, if
God is a God of order, there must also be two deaths, also physical
and spiritual. When God placed Adam in the Garden of Eden and
told him, "Of the tree of the knowledge of good and evil you shall
not eat, for in the day that you eat of it you shall surely die" (Genesis 2:17), He was not speaking metaphorically or allegorically. He
wasn't exaggerating, and He wasn't making idle threats. When the
first husband and wife took bites from the fruit of that tree, death

became a reality. Everything in creation suddenly received an expiration date, including humans.

I've got some bad news and some good news for you. The bad news is that unless you are raptured or God takes you up to heaven in a whirlwind accompanied by a horse and chariot of fire, you are going to die. The good news is that if you are a follower of Jesus Christ, death isn't an event that should cause you any amount of fear.

It used to be that the direction you went after death was the same for everyone—the righteous of God and the unrighteous. In the perfect order of God, He initially sent everybody down.

> The beggar died, and was carried by the angels to Abraham's bosom. The rich man also died and was buried. And being in torments in Hades, he lifted up his eyes and saw Abraham afar off, and Lazarus in his bosom (Luke 16:22-23).

Up until the resurrection of Jesus, everyone went down to Sheol. There, people found themselves in one of two areas, as described in Jesus' account in Luke. For the righteous, there was Abraham's bosom, or Paradise—a place of peace and comfort. For the unrighteous, Hades awaited them, where they would experience great torment. When King Saul went to a medium to consult with the deceased Samuel, the prophet became quite angry and asked, "Why have you disturbed me by bringing me up?" (1 Samuel 28:15). He was grumpily coming "up" from down below in Sheol.

At Jesus' resurrection, changes were made for the location of the believing dead. Before the resurrection, when He was still on the cross, He told the repentant thief, "Assuredly, I say to you, today you will be with Me in Paradise" (Luke 23:43). Remember, that's down below in Sheol. However, after Jesus' resurrection and ascension, Paul told of a new reality. First, we see that the Old Testament souls who were in Abraham's bosom were elevated to heaven:

> When He ascended on high,
> He led captivity captive,
> and gave gifts to men (Ephesians 4:8).

But then Paul also made it clear that from the cross onward, every believer who dies ascends into the presence of the Lord:

> We are always confident, knowing that while we are at home in the body we are absent from the Lord. For we walk by faith, not by sight. We are confident, yes, well pleased rather to be absent from the body and to be present with the Lord (2 Corinthians 5:6-8).

Jesus is not in Sheol. He is at the right hand of the Father in heaven. Therefore, when we die, we know that while our bodies may go down into the ground, our souls go upward into the presence of our Savior in heaven. That is why Paul could be so calm while speaking of his eventual death:

> For to me, to live is Christ, and to die is gain. But if I live on in the flesh, this will mean fruit from my labor; yet what I shall choose I cannot tell. For I am hard-pressed between the two, having a desire to depart and be with Christ, which is far better (Philippians 1:21-23).

Paul was not afraid of dying because he knew that the worst day in heaven is far better than the best day here on earth—and that's assuming that there is any day in heaven that could be described as "the worst." I'm not encouraging anyone to kill themselves, and if you are at all considering that, then please contact your church and get help. We should *always* choose life. We simply need to remember that for the believer, the options are great no matter what happens to us. Living here means fruitful service for the Lord's kingdom and more time with family and friends. Leaving here means experiencing the presence of almighty God. That's called a win-win situation.

That scenario, however, is for the believer only. For the unbeliever, there is no win in death. The first death is terrible because the soul moves to the torment portion of Hades. No matter how one may have suffered here on earth, the justified suffering for one's sins in Sheol is worse. But that is only the first death.

For those who reject Jesus as their Savior, there is a second death awaiting them. Again, with the two births, all are born physically, and believers are born spiritually. With the two deaths, all die physically, and unbelievers die spiritually. When I speak of those who die spiritually, I am referring to those who will be part of the coming second death. For now, sin has killed everyone spiritually, causing a separation from God. It is at our spiritual birth that we who are spiritually dead are made alive, bringing about our new life and our reconciliation with the Father.

The second death doesn't touch those who belong to Christ. John wrote, "Blessed and holy is he who has part in the first resurrection. Over such the second death has no power" (Revelation 20:6). We'll get to the first and second resurrections next, but this is referring to followers in Jesus the Messiah, who should have no fear over the second death. It will not touch them.

What is this second death? It is a complete and permanent disconnection from the love and the presence of God forever. There is no longer any ability to ever be in His company again. That is the consequence of a lack of repentance and a continued life of rebellion against God. Jesus, in His role of Judge, said to John, "The cowardly, unbelieving, abominable, murderers, sexually immoral, sorcerers, idolaters, and all liars shall have their part in the lake which burns with fire and brimstone, which is the second death" (Revelation 21:8). This is Jesus Himself warning of this eternity apart from Him.

What does this "forever apart from God" look like? To understand that, we need to look at the resurrections. You will likely not be surprised to find out that in God's perfect order, there are two of those also.

Order in Restoration—Two Resurrections

Every person is eternal. When God created humanity, He created us in His image. That doesn't mean that we resemble Him physically. As we heard Jesus say to the Samaritan woman, "God is Spirit, and those who worship Him must worship in spirit and truth" (John 4:24). Because God is Spirit, He has no corporeal body. Jesus confirmed this after His resurrection when He said, "A spirit does not have flesh and bones as you see I have" (Luke 24:39). So, when we read of seeing God's face or form, that's called an anthropomorphism, a 16-letter word that just means using human descriptions to try to understand God better.

As part of His image that God has given to us, we are all spiritual beings. The difference is that God is *only* spirit, while we are spirit and flesh. While the flesh part of us is mortal, the spirit part is eternal. This creates a problem, because unlike the Spirit of God, our spirits are designed to function best within a physical body. But an eternal soul in a temporal body? That union can't last forever. When the two are severed, that is called physical death.

What is a spirit like without its fleshly shell? We don't know. It's more than just a ghost floating around. Jesus' earlier telling of the rich man and Lazarus going to Sheol offers as many questions as it does answers. Even in spirit form, the rich man recognized the beggar he had always looked down upon. He also had some sort of bodily structure because he asked, "Father Abraham, have mercy on me, and send Lazarus that he may dip the tip of his finger in water and cool my tongue; for I am tormented in this flame" (Luke 16:24). An unresurrected spirit with a tongue, asking for water from another unresurrected spirit's fingertip? I must admit, I don't fully get it. But that's okay. If God had wanted us to know what a bodiless spirit looks like, the Bible would have been a picture book. I figure I'll learn the answer to that mystery firsthand someday.

Like a hermit crab can function without a shell, a spirit can function without a body. However, that is not how we were designed. So, ultimately, every dead, bodiless person will be transformed in two ways. The dead will be made alive, and they will be given a new, upgraded, immortal body in which they may experience that life. This is called resurrection. Paul wrote about this process, saying, "The body is sown in corruption, it is raised in incorruption" (1 Corinthians 15:42). In other words, like a seed, the body is put into the ground to return to dust. However, when resurrection comes, what will be harvested is a new body that will never die. All in perfect order. What will this process look like? Let's look at the two resurrections described in Scripture.

Everyone should want to be part of the first resurrection, which is occurring in phases over a long period of time. While describing the time of the second coming, John wrote, "Blessed and holy is he who has part in the first resurrection. Over such the second death has no power, but they shall be priests of God and of Christ, and shall reign with Him a thousand years" (Revelation 20:6). The first resurrection is made up only of believers. Remember that the second death brings eternal separation from God in hell. We who take part in the first resurrection never need to fear that eventuality. Instead, we will be priests and judges, and we will reign with our Savior during the 1,000 years of the millennial kingdom.

The first resurrection began in the garden tomb 2,000 years ago. Other people had been raised back to life, but they had all died again because they were not resurrected into their new, incorruptible bodies. Raised from the dead does not equal resurrection. When Jesus returned from the grave, He initiated the first resurrection, one that includes a physical transformation from corruptible into incorruptible.

> Now Christ is risen from the dead, and has become the firstfruits of those who have fallen asleep. For since by man came death, by Man also came the resurrection of the dead. For as in Adam all die, even so in Christ all shall be made alive. But each one in his own order: Christ the firstfruits, afterward those who are Christ's at His coming (1 Corinthians 15:20-23).

Notice Paul laying out the order of God's plan. The body in which Jesus was raised is one that allowed Him to appear and disappear and to pass through walls. Yet it was evident that it was still a real body, brilliantly demonstrated by the Savior when He ate with the disciples. This is also the body that allowed Him to ascend into heaven, where He is seated at the right hand of the Father, as Stephen affirmed at his martyrdom:

> [Stephen], being full of the Holy Spirit, gazed into heaven and saw the glory of God, and Jesus standing at the right hand of God, and said, "Look! I see the heavens opened and the Son of Man standing at the right hand of God!" (Acts 7:55-56).

Right now, Jesus is the only one who is wearing Body 2.0. But that will change, quite possibly very soon, as we will now see.

The second set of recipients of the resurrected body are the church-age saints. If you are a follower of Jesus Christ, then I'm talking about you. We'll discuss the rapture at length in a subsequent chapter, but that glorious event is part of the first resurrection. Similar to the launch of a new car, Jesus was the prototype, rolling out the new model. When we go to meet Him in the clouds, the Lord is going to start His delivery of the new product to the public.

> Behold, I tell you a mystery: We shall not all sleep, but we shall all be changed—in a moment, in the twinkling of an eye, at the last trumpet. For the trumpet will sound, and the dead will be raised incorruptible, and we shall be changed. For this corruptible must put on incorruption, and this mortal must put on immortality. So when this corruptible has put on incorruption, and this mortal has put on immortality, then shall be brought to pass the saying that is written: "Death is swallowed up in victory."

> "O Death, where is your sting?
> O Hades, where is your victory?"
> (1 Corinthians 15:51-55).

I can't read that without getting a smile on my face! Can you imagine what it will be like? First, all those believers who have passed away from the church's first-century advent until today will be raised to receive their resurrections bodies. Why do they go first? Because God is a God of order, and this is the process that He has determined. As Paul wrote, "We who are alive and remain until the coming of the Lord will by no means precede those who are asleep" (1 Thessalonians 4:15). So, relax and wait your turn. After they have all arrived to meet Jesus in the clouds, then those of us who are still alive and part of God's family will be caught up and transformed. What about all the Old Testament saints? Hold on—their time is coming.

The next inductees into the First Resurrection Club number only two. Two witnesses will appear in Jerusalem during the tribulation. They will quickly become the burr in everybody's sock, constantly telling everyone that they are sinners destined for hell. Not surprisingly, their message won't go over well, and people will try to kill them. However, they will be protected by God's hand until they finish the task assigned to them. At that point, the Lord will allow them to be killed. But not to worry.

> After the three-and-a-half days the breath of life from God entered them, and they stood on their feet, and great fear fell on those who saw them. And they heard a loud voice from heaven saying to them, "Come up here." And they ascended to heaven in a cloud, and their enemies saw them (Revelation 11:11-12).

Three-and-a-half days after they are killed, while everyone is holding their Two Dead Witnesses parties, these two servants of God will be resurrected. Then, in their own slow-motion rapture, they will wave goodbye to the people on earth and ascend to heaven, where they will be with the Lord.

The next group of people who will take part in the first resurrection won't arise until the end of the tribulation, when it will be time for the Messiah to return to reign over the earth from Jerusalem. It is at the second coming that we will finally see the resurrection of the Old Testament saints. This is what was promised to Daniel by the man in linen who said to him, "Go your way till the end; for you shall rest, and will arise to your inheritance at the end of the days" (Daniel 12:13). The man told the prophet that although he was going to die like everyone else, there is a resurrection that is awaiting him. Isaiah beautifully described this event, writing,

> Your dead shall live;
> together with my dead body they shall arise.
> Awake and sing, you who dwell in dust;
> for your dew is like the dew of herbs,
> and the earth shall cast out the dead (Isaiah 26:19).

There is one more group of the dead in this first resurrection, whom "the earth shall cast out" at the second coming of Christ. These are the tribulation martyrs. Great news: There is still hope for those who are left behind at the rapture! God's mercy will extend beyond the removal of the church, as we'll see later in this chapter. Those who receive Christ after the rapture will have to endure the horrors of the tribulation and persecution from the antichrist. However, because they have put their faith in the true Savior, they will experience the second birth, which will save them from the second death and will allow them to be part of the first resurrection. Yes, God's order is perfect in all things.

So far, the resurrections described have been nothing but good. But remember, everybody will be resurrected eventually. Jesus said, "Do not marvel at this; for the hour is coming in which all who are in the graves will hear His voice and come forth—those who have done good, to the resurrection of life, and those who have done evil, to the resurrection of condemnation" (John 5:28-29). The spirit is eternal, and it needs an incorruptible body. There are two groups that will be part of a second resurrection that will take place at the end of the millennium. The first are all the mortal believers who died during the 1,000-year reign of Christ. The second—and vastly larger—group will be the unbelievers from all time. This is the "resurrection of condemnation" that Jesus spoke of. These unbelievers will be raised for one purpose alone. They must receive their incorruptible bodies so that they may stand before God, be judged, and receive the just punishment for their sins.

Order in Justice–Seven Future Judgments

The Bible tells us that a time will come when every person will stand before God to face final judgment. It is part of God's natural order: "As it is appointed for men to die once, but after this the judgment" (Hebrews 9:27). What Scripture makes clear, though, is that there is not just one judgment for all people. In fact, there is a series of seven judgments, all of them taking place after the rapture of the church. For the sake of time, I am not going to dive too deeply into any of these judgments, except the first and the last.

1. The Bema Seat Judgment

We lead off with the judgment seat of Christ. Also known as the bema seat judgment, it is only for the church and will take place after we are taken up to be with Jesus. Does this mean that once we get to heaven and see the mansions prepared for us, we're going to have to stand before God to see whether we get to stay or we'll be evicted? Is Peter standing at the pearly gates checking a list of names to see if those in the raptured masses will actually be admitted? Not at all. If you are in heaven, that is where you will stay—at least until the Lord says that it is time to follow Him back to earth.

This judgment is not about punishment, because there is no punishment left for the church. The bema is about rewards. Paul wrote, "We must all appear before the judgment seat of Christ, that each one may receive the things done in the body, according to what he has done, whether good or bad" (2 Corinthians 5:10). This verse was written to the church and talks about what we have done on earth with the gifts and the calling that God has given to us.

The Bible says that

> each one's work will become clear; for the Day will declare it, because it will be revealed by fire; and the fire will test each one's work, of what sort it is. If anyone's work which he has built on it endures, he will receive a reward. If anyone's work is burned, he will suffer loss; but he himself will be saved, yet so as through fire (1 Corinthians 3:13-15).

Once again, this is a reward judgment, not a salvation judgment. Paul greatly anticipated the day he would stand before the judgment seat, telling his protégé Timothy that he couldn't wait to receive "the crown of righteousness, which the Lord, the righteous Judge, will give to me on that Day, and not to me only but also to all who have loved His appearing" (2 Timothy 4:8).

Why do we labor and toil for the Lord with the time we have left on this earth? Why not just kick our feet up and relax, knowing that our salvation has been taken care of by Jesus' work on the cross? We are diligent to carry out our kingdom mission in order to bring glory to God and to show Him how much we love Him. We do it out of worship and obedience and gratitude. We do it because if we truly have a changed life, we know that nothing will bring us greater joy than serving our God. But we also do it because God has given us this little incentive program. By serving Him with our whole hearts, we are earning for ourselves crowns of righteousness that will be given to us at the bema seat judgment. Once again, we are faced with a win-win proposition!

2. The Judgment of Old Testament Believers

The second judgment is that of the Old Testament believers. They will be resurrected at the second coming, after the tribulation. At that point, according to God's perfect order, they will be rewarded for their faithfulness during their lifetimes so long ago. "And all these, having obtained a good testimony through faith, did not receive the promise, God having provided something better for us, that they should not be made perfect apart from us" (Hebrews 11:39-40). Once the church has been rewarded, then it will finally be time for the Old Testament saints to receive what was promised to them.

3. The Judgment of Tribulation Believers

Third in the judgment order comes the tribulation believers. They will be resurrected at the second coming along with the saints of the Old Testament.

> I saw thrones, and they sat on them, and judgment was committed to them. Then I saw the souls of those who had been beheaded for their witness to Jesus and for the word of God, who had not worshiped the beast or his image, and had not received his mark on their foreheads or on their hands. And they lived and reigned with Christ for a thousand years. But the rest of the dead did not live again until the thousand years were finished. This is the first resurrection (Revelation 20:4-5).

It is at this point—following the tribulation—that every believer who has passed away from all times will have been resurrected and received their resurrection bodies. Jesus will sit as a judge in Jerusalem, and they will stand before Him to receive their reward.

After all the believing dead have been dealt with, the question remains: What will happen to the living believers who survive the tribulation, both Jew and Gentile? We will deal with them separately.

4. The Judgment of Living Israel

The fourth judgment in our list is that of living Israel. Through the prophet Ezekiel, God tells His chosen people that after uniting them once again from all the nations, "I will bring you into the wilderness of the peoples, and there I will plead My case with you face to face. Just as I pleaded My case with your fathers in the wilderness of the land of Egypt, so I will plead My case with you" (20:35-36).

The courtroom is set. God is the Judge, and the people of Israel are the defendants. When the case begins, the Judge will set to work. "I will make you pass under the rod, and I will bring you into the bond of the covenant; I will purge the rebels from among you, and those who transgress against Me; I will bring them out of the country where they dwell, but they shall not enter the land of Israel. Then you will know that I am the LORD" (vv. 37-38). The timing of this judgment is unclear. It could be at the beginning of the tribulation, or it could be at the end. Remember, Zechariah 13:8 tells us that ultimately, two-thirds of Israel will be purged, and only one-third will refuse to bow to the antichrist and receive his mark. It is they whom Jesus will bring to Himself at the second coming, and who will receive Him as their Lord and Savior.

5. The Judgment of Living Gentiles

In the fifth judgment, the Gentiles who lived through the tribulation will come before the Judge. God said through the prophet Joel, "I will also gather all nations, and bring them down to the Valley of Jehoshaphat; and I will enter into judgment with them there on account of My people, My heritage Israel" (Joel 3:2). These are obviously not Jews, because they will be judged according to how they treated Israel during the seven years of Jacob's trouble.

Jesus gave us the details of what will happen at this judgment in His description of the separation of the sheep and the goats. He said, "When the Son of Man comes in His glory, and all the holy angels with Him, then He will sit on the throne of His glory. All the nations will be gathered before Him, and He will separate them one from another, as a shepherd divides his sheep from the goats" (Matthew 25:31-32). This obviously refers to the second coming, when Jesus returns in glory. All the Gentiles will gather in the Valley of Jehoshaphat, and they will be separated according to whether they are good sheep or bad goats. Jesus reveals the criteria for determining who is who: Did you show mercy to Me by showing mercy to My people? "Assuredly, I say to you, inasmuch as you did it to one of the least of these My brethren, you did it to Me" (v. 40).

Who are the brethren of Jesus of Nazareth, the one who was born in Bethlehem, of the tribe of Judah? They are the Jews, of course. The assumption in Jesus' parable is that if you are truly a Christian, you will love that which God loves, and God loves the Jews. Do this, and you will show yourself to be a sheep, and you will enter into the millennial kingdom. If you have persecuted the Jews, then you are a goat, and your life will end. You will find yourself in Sheol, where you will await your final judgment.

6. The Judgment of Satan and His Demons

Speaking of final judgment, that is the point in God's order of justice in which we now find ourselves. The sixth judgment is of Satan and all his minions. This comes in two stages. The initial blow is delivered after the battle following the Messiah's second coming:

> Then the beast was captured, and with him the false prophet who worked signs in his presence, by which he deceived those who received the mark of the beast and those who worshiped his image. These two were cast alive into the lake of fire burning with brimstone (Revelation 19:20).

The antichrist and his false prophet will be the first to be tossed into the lake of fire. The devil will be locked away in the abyss to await his release following the millennial reign of Christ. When the 1,000 years have passed, the lid to the abyss will be opened, and Satan will rush to stage his final battle. The enemy and his hordes will be decisively defeated at this second Gog and Magog battle, and the devil will finally receive his due.

> The devil, who deceived them, was cast into the lake of fire and brimstone where the beast and the false prophet are. And they will be tormented day and night forever and ever (Revelation 20:10).

In the battle between good and evil, there was never a doubt as to who would be the victor. The Creator will always defeat the created—a truth the devil forgot, to his own demise.

7. The Great White Throne Judgment

This brings us to our seventh and most tragic of all judgments.

> Then I saw a great white throne and Him who sat on it, from whose face the earth and the heaven fled away. And there was found no place for them. And I saw the dead, small and great, standing before God, and books were opened. And another book was opened, which is the book of life. And the dead were judged according to their works, by the things which were written in the books. The sea gave up the dead who were in it, and Death and Hades delivered up the dead who were in them. And they were judged, each one according to his works. Then Death and Hades were cast into the lake of fire. This is the second death. And anyone not found written in the Book of Life was cast into the lake of fire (Revelation 20:11-16).

I find it painful to even read those words. There are too many people in my past and in my present whom I know will have to stand before God at this judgment.

There will be some—mortal believers who are alive at the end of the millennium—who will stand before God and whose names will be found in the Lamb's book of life. They will receive their incorruptible bodies and will enjoy eternity with the Lord in the new heavens and new earth. However, the vast majority—every unbelieving person from all time who rejected the free offer of salvation through the cross of Christ—will present themselves before the Lord already knowing that their names will not be found written in the Lamb's book of life. What a tragedy!

A TRIBULATION OF MERCY

God's established order needs the tribulation. It is essential for the second birth of the Jews and the judgment of the Gentiles. It is a critical step in the final demise of the great enemy of God and all creation, Satan. But there is one more element to God's order that necessitates this time of tragic turmoil—God's long-suffering mercy.

I know it is difficult to picture the tribulation as being a demonstration of God's mercy. Yet we've already seen how it is through this seven-year trial that all Israel will eventually receive their Messiah. In times of suffering, people will typically react one of two ways. As a result of their pain, some will run away from God, angrily blaming Him for their struggles. Others will run toward Him, seeking His help and strength and mercy.

Peter's second letter was written to Christians under duress; they were suffering persecution from those around them. They were anxious for the return of Christ, wondering why He had not come back yet to save them from their tormentors. But Peter offered them some perspective, writing, "Beloved, do not forget this one thing, that with the Lord one day is as a thousand years, and a thousand years as one day. The Lord is not slack concerning His promise, as some count slackness, but is longsuffering toward us, not willing that any should perish but that all should come to repentance" (2 Peter 3:8-9). It wasn't just the time that allowed for repentance, but the struggles that pushed toward salvation.

How many of those tribulation saints would have been saved without the trials of the tribulation? For some, as soon as the rapture happens, they will realize that all those stories they had heard from their Christian friends are true. For others, it will take devastation after devastation before they will finally turn their hearts to God. Most will never repent, preferring to remain in their state of rebellion. But God is giving humanity seven years of intense suffering in order for them to make that choice.

Has the tribulation begun? No, and thank God that it hasn't. There is still time for friends, family, and, maybe you to give their/ your hearts to Jesus Christ. If you do so now, you will one day be part of the rapture of the church and, thus, guaranteed that you will not have to suffer the day of God's great wrath.

The Lord could have bypassed the tribulation. He could have just said, "I'm tired of you rebels, be you Jew or Gentile. You're destined for hell, so you might as well go now." Instead, He will give one last seven-year reprieve, telling all humanity, "Now is the day of your salvation. Come to Me today. Because very soon it will be too late."

THE DAY OF
DEPARTURE

R *apture.*

This word belongs in the number three position of the "Topics That Have Most Divided the Church," right after COVID vaccinations and the Harry Potter books. Friends have been alienated, pastors and seminary profs have been soundly ridiculed, and congregations have been torn asunder. "You believe in the rapture? Did you know that no one had even heard of a rapture until John Darby in the nineteenth century?" "You *don't* believe in the rapture? Have you ever actually read your Bible?"

Among the scholarly elite, it is likely that more theological fisticuffs have been thrown over this subject than any other in the twentieth and twenty-first centuries. It probably beats out even Replacement Theology versus Dispensationalism and the pre- versus post- versus amillennial debates as the number one topic for countless professorial pay-per-view-level biblical brawls.

But unlike the Replacement/Dispensational and millennial topics, which can sometimes be a little heady, the rapture debate is for the masses. It seems that every Amos, Lev, and Shlomo has their own opinion on the event. Is it real or is it not? If it is real, does it take place before, in the middle of, or after the tribulation? And even within each of those categories, there are a plethora of options—pre-wrath, partial, post. Trying to figure out everyone's stance on the rapture can be a little like trying to nail down the entire office's Starbucks order. "Wait, you're a Ryrie pre-trib, pre-mil dispensationalist with an extra shot of what?" It can get so confusing that many have just thrown up their hands, saying, "How can we ever know?"

When Christians give up on the rapture, it is both sad and a victory for the enemy. The rapture is all about hope in the mercy of God. Satan, who always wants the opposite of what God wants, desires to steal that hope and replace it with fear.

Imagine living in a coastal town. A man approaches you on the street and tells you that a tsunami is about to arrive that will wipe out the entire area. Before you begin to panic, though, he adds, pointing to his left, "But I have a fleet of helicopters in a parking lot one block over. There is room for you and anyone else you can convince to come." What emotions would you feel? Sorrow that the town you love is about to be destroyed? Worry that your friends and neighbors won't accept your invitation to the rescue helicopters? The one emotion you should not experience is fear for your personal safety. Why? You know that you are good because the copters are there waiting to fly you out.

The tribulation is coming. But not only did God provide the means for us to escape it, but He clearly spelled out His plan so that we wouldn't be afraid. That plan is the rapture. The rapture is a wonderful gift from our loving and merciful God that should give us hope and peace. It should also motivate us to let others know how they, too, can escape the coming wrath, and join us in living today without fear of the future.

A BIBLICAL RAPTURE

If you're looking for the best hotels to stay at in Tiberias, the most reasonable restaurants in Eilat, or the fastest route north to Caesarea

Philippi, I'm your man. I was a tour guide long enough that you can trust I won't steer you wrong. However, when it comes to biblical doctrine, you shouldn't trust my words. In fact, you shouldn't trust any person's words. The only word you should trust is God's Word. So, to believe in a rapture just because I say it's true is not good enough. Let's see what the Bible says about it.

As I briefly mentioned in chapter 1, the rapture is a biblical concept. It is not a new idea dreamed up by dispensationalists in order to justify their eschatology. *Eschatology* is the seminary-sized word for "end-times beliefs." In the original Greek New Testament is the word *harpazo*, which means "to snatch, seize, carry away." It is used 14 times in the New Testament, five of those instances referring to a supernatural moving of a person from one location to another.

When the word is used in the instance of Philip, it is clear that after he had finished baptizing the Ethiopian eunuch, the Spirit of the Lord snatched him up out of the water and deposited him elsewhere:

> Now when they came up out of the water, the Spirit of
> the Lord caught Philip away, so that the eunuch saw him
> no more; and he went on his way rejoicing. But Philip
> was found at Azotus (Acts 8:39-40).

This same spiritual "being caught up" is found in the sign of the woman, the child, and the dragon described in Revelation 12. After the woman gave birth, her child was supernaturally "caught up to God and His throne" (v. 5).

Another man who was "caught up" into heaven was the apostle Paul:

> I know a man in Christ who fourteen years ago—whether
> in the body I do not know, or whether out of the body
> I do not know, God knows—such a one was caught up
> to the third heaven. And I know such a man—whether

> in the body or out of the body I do not know, God
> knows—how he was caught up into Paradise and heard
> inexpressible words, which it is not lawful for a man to
> utter (2 Corinthians 12:2-4).

I've heard people try to disqualify that passage. "How do we even know that Paul was describing himself? Why would he be so coy? Besides, from the wording, this could just be some vision that Paul was experiencing." My response is, "And…?" I believe that it is Paul, and that he was granted the privilege of entering the throne room of God. But even if it was just a vision that maybe happened to Paul's cousin Oren who lived in a suburb of Antioch, how does that change the meaning of the phrase "caught up"? The man was on Earth, then suddenly he's snatched up to heaven. Those facts are unimpeachable.

So, when we look at the event described in 1 Thessalonians 4 of Christians being "caught up" to meet Jesus in the clouds, how can we interpret *harpazo* as being anything other than a supernatural snatching up of the church by the Spirit of the Lord?

> The Lord Himself will descend from heaven with a shout,
> with the voice of an archangel, and with the trumpet of
> God. And the dead in Christ will rise first. Then we who
> are alive and remain shall be caught up together with
> them in the clouds to meet the Lord in the air. And thus
> we shall always be with the Lord (1 Thessalonians 4:16-17).

Here, Paul used that Greek word *harpazo*, which was translated into Latin as *rapturo*, from which we derive our English word *rapture*. Some biblical critics and liberal theologians will say, "Oh, 1 Thessalonians is just Paul writing again, as are three of your five 'snatched up' usages. Jesus never believed in a rapture. This is obviously a Pauline addition."

Allow me a moment to remove my palm from my face. If this is your stance, your issue is not with me, but with the Bible. There is one truth—God's truth. There is no Paul's truth and Peter's truth and John's truth and Aunt Gertie's truth. The Bible is a book of truth, and that truth is consistent from cover to cover. Paul will never contradict Jesus, nor will Peter ever contradict Moses. If every example I give to support a point is from the tiny book written by the prophet Obadiah, it doesn't make it any less true or consistent with the rest of Scripture.

If your concern instead is that this is too limited a selection from which to build a doctrine, you should know that not every instance of a snatching away uses this specific word. Enoch, the great-grandfather of Noah, "walked with God; and he was not, for God took him" (Genesis 5:24). The prophet Elijah and his heir apparent, Elisha, were strolling along on the far side of the Jordan when "suddenly a chariot of fire appeared with horses of fire, and separated the two of them; and Elijah went up by a whirlwind into heaven" (2 Kings 2:11). Jesus, after His resurrection, took the disciples to the Mount of Olives. After blessing them, "He was parted from them and carried up into heaven" (Luke 24:51).

There may have been different speeds and varying methods, but each episode held in common the fact that a person was on the earth, he was snatched up by the Spirit of the Lord, and, other than the case of Philip, he ended up in heaven. This is the process that we in the church are promised in 1 Thessalonians 4.

Imagine that you are sitting in your favorite chair at home. You reach for the TV remote, feel a little buzz in your body, then suddenly you are moving. But your trajectory is not horizontal or downward as is normal in a world of gravity. Instead, you are racing upward, past the ceiling and through the roof, which in itself is a little weird as you cannot remember ever having gone through a solid object before without leaving behind a very clear sign of your passage. As you fly, you realize that your body feels different. All those aches and pains of age are completely gone. You haven't felt this good since your twenties. As your gaze leaves your shrinking house, you look up to your destination. You know who's waiting for you. You know that you're about to experience what you've dreamed of ever since you knelt next to your bed years ago and received Jesus as your Lord and Savior. Then you see Him, and suddenly the world below you is gone, and the millions who are flying up around you fade away. It's just you and Him as He opens His arms to receive you.

Is that what it will be like at the rapture? Maybe, maybe not. All that looking around would probably have to occur in a fraction of a second, which isn't likely. But it's still fun to think about. The things that God doesn't make clear in Scripture are open grounds for our fertile imaginations as long as we always make sure that the scriptural truth bucket and the imagination bucket never let their contents mix. What we do know is that the rapture will be a once-in-an-eternity experience for us, and it will be spectacular. If that doesn't bring you joy and hope, then your joy and hope generator needs a tune-up!

Why a Rapture?—Saved from Wrath

With the fact of the rapture established, we can now move on to the most important question: Why? Sure, it's an amazing event and it certainly sounds like a lot of fun, but what is the ultimate purpose for the Spirit doing this snatch-and-grab of believers? By determining the reasons for the rapture, much of the "weirdness" of the event will dissipate and be replaced with a feeling of "Oh, well that makes sense." Resolving the *why* question will also unlock the answers to two other critical pieces of information—*who* and *when*. We will touch on the *when* here, but we'll deal with it much more thoroughly in the next chapter.

What have we learned thus far? Mankind's rebellious heart led to sin. The wages of our sin is death—physical and spiritual. Yet God provided a way for us to be spared from spiritual death. Jesus died for us, and through His shed blood, we can have our sins washed away. This free gift is available for all who will take it. Right now, God is in a holding pattern of long-suffering patience waiting for more and more to choose eternal life in Him. Eventually, though, His patience will end, and He will pour out His wrath. The wrath will be unleashed for two primary reasons: first, to discipline the Jews to repentance, and second, to punish those who continue in their rebellion against Him. Then there is one more product of the tribulation that we can surmise. In a glorious act of God's great mercy, the seven years of tribulation will give Gentiles one last opportunity to come to Him.

When it comes to those three reasons, where do believers fit in? Reasons one and three don't work, because whether Jew or Gentile, a true Christian has already repented and come to salvation through faith in Jesus Christ. Would the tribulation cause us to repent even further and get even more saved than we were before? That obviously doesn't make any sense. Being saved is like being pregnant—you either are or you aren't.

That leaves us with reason two: the punishment for rebellion. This is where some Christians speak up. They believe that the church needs to go through the tribulation for one of two purposes. Some look at today's church and say, "We are so far from the purity of the first-century church, and we have allowed so much sin into the church by lowering our standards of morality that we deserve to go through the seven years of disciplinary suffering." But first, take some time to read Revelation chapters 2 and 3, and maybe peruse the book of 1 Corinthians. The first-century church wasn't all that pure.

As for our lowering standards, that may or may not be true. I tend to think that the true church is in a pretty good place. Remember, not every organization that calls itself a church is part of the true church. I could call myself the greatest football forward ever, but that doesn't mean I'm ever going to steal Cristiano Ronaldo's roster spot. The church is made up of people, not buildings or denominations. There are many congregations who gather in "church" buildings on Sunday to listen to vapid sermons supported occasionally by out-of-context Scripture passages. People do this so they can feel better about their morally bankrupt lives. They gravitate to those servants of Satan who call themselves pastors and tell them that all that matters is that they are true to themselves. This is not the church.

The church is made up of followers of Jesus Christ who are still living in this sin-tainted world wearing these bodies of lustful flesh. Thus, there will always be Christians at all levels of spiritual commitment. Some will be passionate for the Lord, others will be good and consistent servants in their local body, and others will get by, "but only as through fire" (1 Corinthians 3:15 ESV). The one hope that each believer has is that they are a sinner saved by grace, with all sins—past, present, and future—already dealt with by Jesus on the cross. Because our sins have all been dealt with, there is no reason for us to experience a seven-year purgatorial cleansing here on Earth. Our transgressions are gone.

There is also no reason to "purify" the church, the bride, before her upcoming nuptials to Jesus Christ, the Groom, as some are wont to say. They point to Paul's words to the Corinthians—"I am jealous for you with godly jealousy. For I have betrothed you to one husband, that I may present you *as* a chaste virgin to Christ" (2 Corinthians 11:2)—and they say, "The church is not a chaste virgin right now, so we must be purified through the tribulation." I am not a biologist or a medical doctor, but I can safely state that no amount of suffering or tribulation is going to revert a nonvirgin back into a virgin.

Others look to Ephesians 5, saying that the way Jesus will "sanctify and cleanse" His bride is through the tribulation. But we need to look at the full context:

> Husbands, love your wives, just as Christ also loved the church and gave Himself for her, that He might sanctify and cleanse her with the washing of water by the word, that He might present her to Himself a glorious church, not having spot or wrinkle or any such thing, but that she should be holy and without blemish (vv. 25-27).

The context is marriage, and Paul said that husbands should follow the example of Christ. If Jesus is going to purify His bride through the tribulation, then does that mean that the best way for Christian husbands to sanctify and cleanse their wives is through suffering and violence? Perish the thought!

What was Paul saying? The answer is right in the text. The sanctifying and cleansing will be done through "the washing of water by the word." In the same way that Jesus has led the church to greater sanctification through His sacrifice and His spiritual leadership through His teachings, a husband will lead his wife to a deeper walk with the Lord through his personal sacrifice for her and his commitment to being the spiritual leader in the home—one who is committed to teaching the Bible through action and word. Truly, it takes a truckload of bad biblical interpretation to see the tribulation in either of those passages.

What it comes down to is that despite our occasional rebellions and sinful actions, we who are believers are not destined to wrath.

> God did not appoint us to wrath, but to obtain salvation through our Lord Jesus Christ, who died for us, that whether we wake or sleep, we should live together with Him (1 Thessalonians 5:9-10).

There is no *biblical* reason for us to experience God's wrath. There is no *logical* reason for us to experience His wrath. And, because of the completeness of Christ's work on the cross, there is no *spiritual* reason for us to experience His wrath. So, rather than fearing the trials that are soon to come upon Earth, we can, with the Thessalonians, "wait for His Son from heaven, whom He raised from the dead, even Jesus who delivers us from the wrath to come" (1 Thessalonians 1:10).

Why a Rapture?—To Be with Jesus

On the night that Jesus was arrested, He and the disciples were reclining in an upper room. The flickering flames from the oil lamps were enough to illuminate those around the table, although the corners of the room were likely dark. It had been a good but somewhat odd night. During the meal, Jesus had suddenly gotten up and washed all their feet, telling them that He was setting an example for how they should view one another. Then He began talking about betrayal, which turned into Judas suddenly leaving the room.

Next, Jesus began telling them to love each other because He was about to go away to a place that was apparently off-limits to the rest of them. No surprise—Peter was having none of it. "Wherever You're going to go, I'm going to go. You need my protection, and I'll lay down my life for You." That was so Peter. But then Jesus turned it all around with a blow that sucked the air out of the room. He told Peter that this very night, he was going to deny Him three times.

You could have heard a pin drop in the room. Everyone's eyes were on Peter's red face as he shook with sorrow and rage. Then Jesus cleared His throat, and they all turned to Him. He smiled with a reassuring smile that said, "It doesn't matter if a whole Roman legion is coming after you; I've got you." Immediately, the tension left the room, and He said to them as well as to us:

> Let not your heart be troubled; you believe in God, believe
> also in Me. In My Father's house are many mansions; if
> *it* were not so, I would have told you. I go to prepare a

place for you. And if I go and prepare a place for you, I will come again and receive you to Myself; that where I am, there you may be also (John 14:1-3).

What amazing words the Lord spoke to His disciples, and, ultimately, to us in the church! First, Jesus said that He was going to prepare a place for them. What does that tell you? It means that He was going to leave them, but there will come a day when they will join Him at the location to which He was going.

Imagine if I were to tell my lovely wife that I am going to Haifa on the Mediterranean, where I will build a perfect little vacation home. I will give her a big kitchen, and I will decorate it in the style that I've come to know she loves after our many years of marriage. Once I complete the work and the little beach house is ready, she will naturally ask me, "When do I get to see it?" What sense would it make if I told her, "Oh, it's not for you to stay in. I just thought you'd be happy knowing it's there."

When Jesus said that He was preparing a place for the disciples, the logical conclusion is that He will one day take them to that place so they can enjoy the fruits of His labor.

Jesus also told them that He will come again. He is not just going to text them an address to plug into their smartphones for directions. He's not sending a car or a party bus to pick them up. He is personally making the round trip. Jesus is leaving them, then Jesus is coming back for them.

What will He do when He comes again? He will receive them to Himself. They will not receive Him to themselves. Jesus is not coming to Earth, where everyone has prepared a place for Him. There will be no "Welcome Home" barbecue with a live band and fireworks. Instead, it's just the opposite. Remember what Paul wrote about this occasion: "Then we who are alive and remain shall be caught up together with them in the clouds to meet the Lord in the air. And thus we shall always be with the Lord" (1 Thessalonians 4:17). He is coming in the clouds, and then we will go to Him.

Notice Jesus' last phrase in the John passage and Paul's last phrase in the words just above. They are essentially saying the same thing. "Where I am, that's where you will be. And that's how it's going to be forever." Once again, Jesus is not saying, "Where you are, there I'll be." He's not the passive person in the relationship. He's not going to follow us around so that we can always be together. No, we are meeting Him in the clouds so that we may go to where He is residing. Where is that? Heaven, of course, where He has gone to prepare a place for us.

Praise the Lord! Once the rapture occurs, not only the disciples, but the entire church will be with Jesus forever. That is why Paul could write this blessing:

> May the Lord make you increase and abound in love to one another and to all, just as we do to you, so that He may establish your hearts blameless in holiness before our God and Father at the coming of our Lord Jesus Christ with all His saints (1 Thessalonians 3:12-13).

The second coming of Jesus to Earth is not the same as the rapture. Unless your picture of the church meeting Jesus in the clouds is like riding to the top of the escalator, only to take two steps over and ride it right back down, then a rapture/second coming combo makes absolutely no logical sense. We will be taken up to be with Jesus, and He will take us to be with Him at the place that He has prepared for us. Then when it is time for His return to Earth, He will come back with us, the church, referred to above as "all His saints."

Why a Rapture?—To Carry Out the Bema Seat Judgment

We examined this event in the previous chapter. It is the reward judgment for the church. How do we know that the bema seat isn't just another way to refer to the Great White Throne, which is the ultimate salvation judgment? Let's just look one more time at what Paul says about the bema, translated here as "judgment seat":

> We make it our aim, whether present or absent, to be well pleasing to Him. For we must all appear before the judgment seat of Christ, that each one may receive the things done in the body, according to what he has done, whether good or bad (2 Corinthians 5:9-10).

Paul says that we want to do right for the Lord. We want to serve Him and live the way He wants us to live so that we can be "well pleasing to Him." Like children who want to make their fathers proud, so we seek the approval of Jesus the Messiah. Then he introduces the word "for." This means Paul is about to give us an explanation. "We live well pleasing to Him, for/because/since this is true." In that second sentence, he wrote that we strive to serve and live for Jesus, for we know that a judgment is coming.

This is why the bema cannot be a salvation judgment. Otherwise, Paul would be saying that we live righteously because we know that a judgment is coming, and if we don't meet God's behavioral standards, then we're destined for hell. That is pure works salvation. We might as well be under the law because Jesus will have died for nothing.

No, our salvation is not based on anything that we do, before or after we receive Him as our Lord and Savior. We can't be good enough to earn salvation, and we can't be bad enough to lose it. Otherwise, salvation becomes a "me" thing, not a Jesus thing. "I earn my redemption, and it is up to my good behavior to hang on to it." That is not the gospel of Jesus. As the old hymn goes, "My hope is built on nothing less than Jesus' blood and righteousness."

It is only through faith in Jesus that we will receive the grace, mercy, and forgiveness that bring salvation. The Great White Throne is the salvation judgment when the books will be opened. The bema is when the people who make up the church will receive their rewards for their holy service to the Lord.

So, as the church, we wait for the day when we hear the voice of God blasting for us to join Him. I use the term *blasting* for a reason. What did John hear when he was called up to heaven to witness the events of Revelation? "After these things I looked, and behold, a door standing open in heaven. And the first voice which I heard was like a trumpet speaking with me, saying, 'Come up here, and I will show you things which must take place after this'" (Revelation 4:1). What does a trumpet do? It calls people to attention with the intensity and volume of its sounding. The voice John heard had that kind of intensity when it summoned him, saying, "Come up here!"

This is the same powerful voice that will resound at the resurrection of the two witnesses, giving out the same call: "They heard a loud voice from heaven saying to them, 'Come up here.' And they ascended to heaven in a cloud, and their enemies saw them" (Revelation 11:12). Who is behind this powerful, trumpet-like directive? It is the Lord Himself, as Paul informs us, writing, "For the Lord Himself will descend from heaven with a shout, with the voice of an archangel, and with the trumpet of God" (1 Thessalonians 4:16). What is the trumpet of God? It is the Lord's voice calling to His church to "come up here" and join Him for all eternity.

When does this rewards judgment happen? It can't be during this lifetime. I know of no one who has received a summons to appear before this spiritual court. Yet it also has to be before the church returns with Christ. When John described the bride's return to earth with the Groom, he wrote, "To her it was granted to be arrayed in fine linen, clean and bright, for the fine linen is the righteous acts of the saints" (Revelation 19:8). This describes a church whose actions have already been judged, and those acts of service declared to be righteous have been rewarded.

Thus, the bema has to be between the time of the rapture and the second coming. Jesus Himself confirmed this as He closed the Scriptures, saying, "Behold, I am coming quickly, and My reward is with Me, to give to everyone according to his work" (Revelation 22:12). When Jesus comes in the clouds to meet His church, He will be fully prepared to reward each person for their righteous acts at the coming bema judgment.

Why a Rapture?—To Ring the Wedding Bells

I can still picture my wife walking down the aisle to join me at our wedding. She was so beautiful, and I was overwhelmed that this woman was coming forward to choose me to be her husband. It's likely that most of you who are married can remember your aisle moment also. Either you were the groom at the front watching your bride come to you, or you were the bride walking forward to give yourself to your husband. It is a sacred, solemn, and joyous time.

That is a picture of the rapture. We read earlier Paul's words about wanting to present to Jesus the church as a chaste virgin. This is that moment of presentation. We, the bride, are coming forward to be with our Groom. And as God intended with human marriage, once we are with our Groom, we will never be apart again.

There is debate as to whether the actual marriage will take place in heaven or on earth. John described the event, writing,

> I heard, as it were, the voice of a great multitude, as the sound of many waters and as the sound of mighty thunderings, saying, "Alleluia! For the Lord God Omnipotent reigns! Let us be glad and rejoice and give Him glory, for the marriage of the Lamb has come, and His wife has made herself ready." And to her it was granted to be arrayed

in fine linen, clean and bright, for the fine linen is the
righteous acts of the saints. Then he said to me, "Write:
'Blessed are those who are called to the marriage supper
of the Lamb!'" (Revelation 19:6-9).

It makes sense that the marriage will take place in heaven. Jesus
will call His bride to Himself. He will provide places for her to live.
The bride will return with Him to earth at the second coming. Also,
think about how Jesus will look when He returns. As we saw before
in Revelation 19:11-16, He will come back as the Warrior King, ready
to judge the world. His robe will be dipped in blood, and a sword will
proceed from His mouth. I know that there are many marriage cus-
toms around this world, but I'm guessing that this would be unique.

As for the celebration feast, it may follow up in heaven with the
yet-to-be resurrected Old Testament saints as the blessed guests. Or
it may take place on earth with all those who are not of the church
but are part of the first resurrection in attendance, including the now-
resurrected Old Testament saints and tribulation martyrs. Much of
the debate of the timing and location of the wedding feast comes
from the story Jesus told in Matthew 22.

After the triumphal entry, the Pharisees and spiritual leaders came
after Jesus full force. With every new sortie, they were shot down.
In the midst of these attacks, Jesus told a parable, beginning, "The
kingdom of heaven is like a certain king who arranged a marriage
for his son, and sent out his servants to call those who were invited
to the wedding; and they were not willing to come" (Matthew 22:2-
3). Person after person gave their excuses as to why they were unable
to attend this special event. So the king sent out more servants with
more invites, and this time the people of the city abused and even
killed the messengers. Upon hearing of their mistreatment of his servants, the king, in a rage, killed the murderers and burned the city.

With justice having been brought against those unworthy people, the king was still facing a problem. He had a wedding feast ready, but no one left on the guest list. So he told his servants, "The wedding is ready, but those who were invited were not worthy. Therefore go into the highways, and as many as you find, invite to the wedding" (vv. 8-9). Soon the wedding hall was full.

But that's not the end of the story. When the king came to the feast, he spotted a man who was not wearing the proper clothing. The monarch was irate, had him bound, and ordered his servants to "take him away, and cast him into outer darkness; there will be weeping and gnashing of teeth" (v. 13). I will be honest with you. When I was a new Christian, the unexpected ending to this story almost caused me to lose my faith. It seemed so petty and vindictive. However, once I finally understood the parable, it all made sense.

There are many who look at this story as proof that God has rejected Israel. The Jews were invited to the great wedding feast of Revelation 19, but they rejected their invitation. So, God removed them from His plan and instead, invited the Gentile church to take their place. The problem is that the church is not made up of wedding guests. We are the bride! Why would we be receiving invitations to our own wedding?

This parable is speaking instead of God's great plan of salvation, the entrance into the "kingdom of heaven" (v. 2). This is not the wedding feast of the church spoken of in Revelation 19, so we need to get that our of our minds. Not every mention of a wedding feast in the Bible is *the* wedding feast. We've got to look at the context. Here, Jesus was being attacked by the religious leaders, so He told His listeners, "These guys were invited to salvation, but they were too busy with their own stuff and doing things their own way. They wouldn't listen to God's messengers. Therefore, God has rejected the hoity-toity leaders and opened the doors of His kingdom to the masses."

This is the same accusation that Paul leveled against Israel when he wrote:

Brethren, my heart's desire and prayer to God for Israel is that they may be saved. For I bear them witness that they have a zeal for God, but not according to knowledge. For they being ignorant of God's righteousness, and seeking to establish their own righteousness, have not submitted to the righteousness of God. For Christ is the end of the law for righteousness to everyone who believes (Romans 10:1-4).

This is also a description of that guy wearing the wrong clothes. How many people have you seen or heard of, maybe even in your churches, who are doing Christianity "their way"? They have their own special twist on salvation or their relationship with God. They refuse to celebrate God's simple grace as Isaiah did: "I will greatly rejoice in the LORD, my soul shall be joyful in my God; for He has clothed me with the garments of salvation, He has covered me with the robe of righteousness" (Isaiah 61:10). Therefore, the Lord looks at them and says, "I gave one simple plan of salvation, which you refused to wear. That is rebellion, which is sin. Sorry, but you're out of here."

All that to say, we cannot use Matthew 22 to help time the wedding feast, as many do. It's not what Jesus was talking about. So, when and where is the wedding? It is in heaven, *before* we return with the Lord at His second coming. When is the wedding feast? It could either be in heaven during the tribulation or on earth during the millennium. Because the Bible is not crystal clear, I will not be dogmatic. Besides, the exact timing is an ancillary point. What is important to recognize is that at the rapture, Jesus the Groom is coming for His church, the bride. And once we are with Him, our union will remain eternal.

WHO IS THE RAPTURE FOR?

Remember that I said once we understand the *why* of the rapture, we'll know the *who* and the *when*? Again, we'll deal with the timing in the next chapter as we look at the various views. As for the who, let's just review our main points: saved from wrath, taken to be with Jesus, bema seat judgment, and bride of Christ. The rapture is undoubtedly for the church. There is no other entity or group of people who have been blessed with all those promises.

The rapture belongs to the church. It is our Savior's way of removing us from a terrible situation in which we don't belong and taking us to where we do belong. In fact, the place to which He is taking us is one that He has specially prepared for us for that exact time. So, if you are a believer in Jesus Christ, be excited! The time is soon coming when

> the Lord Himself will descend from heaven with a shout, with the voice of an archangel, and with the trumpet of God. And the dead in Christ will rise first. Then we who are alive and remain shall be caught up together with them in the clouds to meet the Lord in the air. And thus we shall always be with the Lord (1 Thessalonians 4:16-17).

A MATTER OF TIMING

There are few things that people of faith love more than finding reasons to divide. Islam has the Sunnis and the Shiites. In Buddhism, you'll find the Theravāda and the Mahāyāna, along with a multitude of other schools of thought. In Christianity, there are as many denominations as the day is long, some of which are strongly evangelical in their beliefs and others that quite possibly have less to do with true Christianity than the Theravāda Buddhists.

The apostle Paul understood this love of division and knew how to exploit it. After he was arrested in Jerusalem, he was brought before the high priests and their council. As he stood before this hostile audience, the Roman commander told him to state his case. Paul knew that there was no way he would get a fair hearing with this crowd. So, instead, he decided to conjure up a little religious controversy:

> When Paul perceived that one part were Sadducees and the other Pharisees, he cried out in the council, "Men and brethren, I am a Pharisee, the son of a Pharisee; concerning the hope and resurrection of the dead I am being judged!" And when he had said this, a dissension arose between the Pharisees and the Sadducees; and the assembly was

divided. For Sadducees say that there is no resurrection—
and no angel or spirit; but the Pharisees confess both. Then
there arose a loud outcry. And the scribes of the Pharisees'
party arose and protested, saying, "We find no evil in this
man; but if a spirit or an angel has spoken to him, let us
not fight against God" (Acts 23:6-9).

This was a brilliant move! Paul knew that the only people these
two groups hated more than him was each other. Once the apostle
reminded them of their doctrinal differences, the Pharisees forgot
all about how much they wanted to kill him and actually began to
defend him. God must shake His head when He sees some of the
divisions that take place between those who profess Him.

Unfortunately, the subject that I am about to bring up now is, in
many circles, akin to yelling "Resurrection!" in a crowd full of Sadducees. When in relation to the tribulation will the rapture occur?
Will it be before the tribulation, during it, throughout it, or after?
At times, the debate can get so contentious that people prefer to not
address this topic at all. "Isn't it unnecessary and kind of petty? It
doesn't really matter what your view is. We'll all find out soon enough."

But it is not a petty discussion. The timing of the rapture is very
important. It tells us much about who God is and how He treats
those who follow Him. It also is a determining factor in how we will
spend the time we have left on this earth. If the rapture could happen at any moment, then we should have a sense of urgency about
how we spend our time. If we know that we have plenty of years left,
that same flame will not be stoked.

Having read this far into the book, it will not surprise you that
I believe in a pre-tribulation rapture, meaning that the rapture will
happen before the tribulation begins. I know that there are many
out there who believe as I do. But quite a few of them don't know
how to defend their belief. The moment they hear a Bible verse that

they don't understand, or someone fallaciously tells them that no one believed in a pre-trib rapture before John Darby came up with the idea in the nineteenth century, they panic or wilt. That's perfectly understandable if you have never studied this subject. My goal in this chapter is for you to understand not just what the other rapture beliefs are, but why the pre-tribulation rapture is the only one that fits both the Scriptures and the character of God.

And just as an aside, I became a believer in a pre-tribulation rapture not because of what anyone taught me, but because I studied the Bible. In fact, once I learned of Darby and read his stuff, I thought, *Wow, he believes like I do. What a smart guy!*

There are five major views for the timing of the rapture: partial, mid-trib, pre-wrath, post-trib, and pre-trib. We'll address them one at a time.

PARTIAL RAPTURE

This view says believers will be raptured throughout the tribulation based on the level of punishment needed to purify them. If you are a great Christian who gives regularly to the church, teaches Sunday school weekly, and passes out gospel tracts instead of candy at Halloween, then you very well might fly straight into heaven with the first batch of believers. However, if you are more of a sin-on-Saturday-pray-on-Sunday Christian, then you might need to go through a few years of suffering so that you can be purified enough to enter the presence of your Savior.

There are many flaws in this view, but three should be enough to disqualify it. First, a partial rapture divides the body of Christ. It creates a tier system, then segments the church based on those levels. It turns the church into the English football pyramid. The Premier League Christians fly first. After a little suffering, the Championship League Christians finally get their relief. The League One members of the church need a little more wrath, so they endure a couple more years. Then finally, at the end, the League Two Christians get raptured, provided they have somehow managed to keep themselves alive that long.

Nowhere does the Bible divide the church like that. Yes, there will be different levels of rewards given at the bema seat judgment, but again, that involves rewards, not punishment. As we saw before, Paul wrote, "We must all appear before the judgment seat of Christ, that each one may receive the things done in the body, according to what he has done, whether good or bad" (2 Corinthians 5:10). Later, in a letter to Timothy, Paul identified the reward given for faithful service as "the crown of righteousness" (2 Timothy 4:8), not time off for good behavior.

That touches on the other two reasons why the partial rapture view doesn't work. As we mentioned before, the tribulation is not some sort of purgatory that requires Christians to suffer just punishments for their sins. Jesus already endured all the suffering needed as He hung on the cross. And finally, the partial rapture view emphasizes too much the power of our works. What we do neither pays the penalty for our sin nor reduces the suffering necessary for our punishment. We can never do enough to impact either one of those accounts. Only Jesus' sacrifice on the cross was powerful enough to wipe out those ledgers.

MID-TRIB RAPTURE

Imagine being in the tribulation. *It's been a strange few years*, you reflect as you put the leg rest up on your recliner. After the insanity of that big battle in Israel when Russia took a major beating, the world settled down. Not that things are the same as they used to be. The citizens of the globe are now much more touchy-feely and see themselves as one world. There's also that one guy who acts like he owns the place—that place being all the nations of the world. You've read your Bible; you've heard the sermons; you know who he is. But he has brought peace. You've got to give him credit for that. As you open a Pepsi and pick up the TV remote, you think, *All in all, the first half of the tribulation hasn't been that bad.*

But you know that's got to come to an end soon. If your pastor's timing is right based on Russia's attack of Israel, then next Thursday will be the day that Jesus comes back in the clouds to take the church to heaven. Part of you thinks that you ought to let your neighbor know what is about to happen now that the really bad part of the tribulation is ready to begin. But next Thursday is nine days away. You've still got time.

The biggest problem with a mid-tribulation view of the rapture is that it misunderstands the nature of the seven years of God's wrath— primarily, that it is actually *seven years* of God's wrath. Those who hold this view will typically say that the first half of the tribulation is not all that bad. When it really gets nasty is during the second three-and-a-half years. However, a quick look at the timeline of Revelation and where the seal judgments of chapter 6 fit in shows that there is bad stuff happening throughout the entire time. If you don't want to wait until chapter 11 of this book, when we will look at the judgments of the tribulation in more detail, then just peruse Revelation 6. Anyone who thinks that the first half of the tribulation will be a cakewalk is sorely mistaken.

Even more important, though, is the fact that there is nowhere in Scripture that clearly indicates a rapture after the first half of the tribulation. The only way to make this view work is to eisegete, which means taking your already-held doctrine and searching for biblical passages that you can use to support your belief. The problem with that method is that you can misinterpret and twist Scripture to support any belief. Just look at how so many racist organizations misuse the Bible to support their abhorrent views. The opposite of eisegesis is exegesis, which looks at Scripture and lets it tell you what to believe. Proper exegesis that uses a literal method of interpretation will nullify any attempt to justify a mid-trib rapture.

PRE-WRATH RAPTURE

While you won't find many Christians who hold to the two pre-vious views, the introduction of the pre-wrath rapture moves us into what we might consider the Big Three. This view has similarities to the mid-trib perspective as far as timing. However, the reasons for holding to a somewhere-in-the-second-half-of-the-tribulation tim-ing for the rapture are different.

For the pre-wrath supporter, there is no distinction between the words *elect*, *saints*, and *church*. For them, the saints who have been elected to salvation by God are all part of the church. So, upon hear-ing that I have made the claim that the church is nowhere mentioned in Revelation 4–19, they'll accost me in my favorite coffee shop and say, "Hold on there, Amir. You better take a second look." Then they'll read to me, "It was granted to him to make war with the saints and to overcome them. And authority was given him over every tribe, tongue, and nation" (Revelation 13:7). Then they'll flip a few chap-ters later and read, "I saw the woman, drunk with the blood of the saints and with the blood of the martyrs of Jesus. And when I saw her, I marveled with great amazement" (17:6).

"Who are the saints," they'll ask, "and who are the martyrs of Jesus, if not the church?"

Then, as I take another sip of my cappuccino, they'll keep going: "Even Jesus said that the church was in the tribulation." Then they'll quote to me Jesus' words from the Olivet Discourse, saying, "Unless those days were shortened, no flesh would be saved; but for the elect's sake those days will be shortened" (Matthew 24:22).

After I put down my cup and dab the corners of my mouth with my napkin, I'll remind them that you can't drop every use of the word "saint" into the church basket. There are Old Testament saints, tribu-lation saints, millennial saints, and, yes, even church saints. While all of them are eventually heaven bound, the timing of their relocation is not the same. It is all part of the various stages of the first resurrection, which we talked about in chapter 4.

The same is true of the word "elect." We've already seen how Peter, in his first epistle, calls the church a "chosen generation" (2:9). When he does, he uses the same Greek word, *eklektos*, translated as "elect" in Matthew 24. This is also the identical word used in the Septuagint, the Greek translation of the Old Testament, to translate God's words about the special relationship between Himself and Israel:

> I will bring forth descendants from Jacob,
> and from Judah an heir of My mountains;
> My elect shall inherit it,
> and My servants shall dwell there (Isaiah 65:9).

Same word, different entities. The context of each use of "saint" and "elect" determines who is being talked about. Not every track athlete is a sprinter, not every dog is a schnauzer, not every saint is a member of the church, and not every elect is part of the bride of Christ.

One more difficulty with the pre-wrath position is the way proponents divide the tribulation period. In order to accommodate the church being saved from wrath, a biblical promise we'll examine under the pre-trib view, many pre-wrath advocates separate the seven years of God's judgment into three sections. First is the beginning of sorrows, during which the seal judgments are opened. Next, comes the great tribulation, at which time the trumpet judgments are sounded. Finally, the day of the Lord dawns. This is when the wrath of God is poured out on the earth in the form of the bowl judgments, and it is from these punishments that the church is rescued.

While each of those identifiers are biblical, there is nothing to indicate that they speak specifically of a certain set of judgments. In fact, the grammar surrounding Jesus' use of the phrase "beginning of sorrows" in Matthew 24:8 implies that it takes place prior to the commencement of the tribulation. Taking scriptural phrases and using them to label unconnected events is shoddy biblical interpretation.

POST-TRIB RAPTURE

The view that the rapture will take place at the end of the tribulation has both hermeneutical and logical problems. Hermeneutics is a fancy term that refers to the rules that you use when interpreting the Bible. Many who hold to the post-tribulation rapture view reject a literal interpretation of Scripture as their standard, and instead, hold wide-open the door to allegorizing. As a result, they say that much, if not all, of what is described by Jesus in Matthew 24 and by John in Revelation already took place during the destruction of Jerusalem in AD 70. They also join many of the pre-wrath proponents in saying that there is little to no difference between Israel and the church.

This view is incompatible with a literal interpretation of the Bible. So many of the events described in the Olivet Discourse and the book of Revelation cannot find direct correlation in the Roman destruction of Jerusalem and the temple by Titus. Therefore, those who hold to a first-century fulfillment must retreat to the hermeneutic of "These words don't mean here what they usually mean everywhere else." Once the allegorical approach to interpreting Scripture becomes a viable option, then it becomes very easy to make the Bible say anything that you want it to say.

The logical problems with the post-trib viewpoint are twofold. First, it is very difficult to determine a reason for the rapture. According to this viewpoint, when Jesus will descend at the second coming, those believers who are still alive at the end of the tribulation will rise up to meet Him in the air alongside all those believers who have previously died. Then Jesus and His great band of followers will all descend back down to earth immediately to usher in the millennium. What is the purpose of this reverse bungee, racing up into the sky so we can race right back down? Did we need to be disconnected from terra firma for our bodies to be changed? Did Jesus want a big aerial audience to watch Him touch down? In a post-trib context, the rapture doesn't make sense.

There is also a logical problem when it comes to who will populate the millennium. If all unbelievers are killed and set aside for future judgment and all believers are raptured and now have their incorruptible bodies, there are no corruptible mortals left. Is that a problem? It is when you factor in the time of Satan's release from the abyss at the end of the 1,000 years. When he returns to earth, he will find a sizable corrupt population who will be ready to join him in one last battle against the kingdom of Christ. With a post-trib rapture, there will be no sinful people left to populate his army.

PRE-TRIB RAPTURE

I have already made clear that it is in this position that my hope lies. When I speak of my hope, it is not in the sense of seeing the first star of the evening and saying, "I wish I may, I wish I might, be raptured away from the tribulation tonight." The reason for my hope rests solely on the Word of God and the promises He has made to the church. Yet I recognize that there are many Christians who either don't believe in the rapture or who think that its timing is other than before the tribulation.

Some argue against the pre-trib view, saying that it is a more recent doctrine. All the church fathers held to something different, they claim. But that is not true. There were many early church writers who held to an imminent, at-any-moment rapture. In AD 373, Ephraem the Syrian wrote, "For all the saints and elect of God are gathered, prior to the tribulation that is to come, and are taken to the Lord lest they see the confusion that is to overwhelm the world because of our sins." Irenaeus, a disciple of Polycarp, who was a disciple of the apostle John, wrote in the second century, "And therefore, when in the end the Church shall be suddenly caught up from this, it is said, 'There shall be tribulation such as has not been since the beginning, neither shall be' (Matthew 24:21)." But even if no church father had mentioned a pre-tribulation rapture, that would not concern me because, as we have seen and will now see again, the Bible clearly teaches that Jesus will come for His bride prior to the wrath of God being poured out on the earth.

Another very popular argument against the pre-trib view is that the church deserves some suffering. In fact, Jesus said that difficult times are going to come. In John 16:33, He told His disciples, "These things I have spoken to you, that in Me you may have peace. In the world you will have tribulation; but be of good cheer, I have overcome the world." But just like not all antichrists are *the* antichrist, not all tribulations are *the* tribulation. The Greek word used here is *thlipsis* and means "trouble, tribulation, oppression, persecution." Jesus could not have been telling His disciples that they would endure the great tribulation, because they didn't. They underwent trouble, oppression, persecution, and, yes, tribulation, but they died long before the seven years of God's judgment on the earth.

"But, Amir, look how easy the Western church has it," some say. "The greatest trial most of us have is when the espresso machine is down at the Holy Roaster's coffee bar in the lobby." First, watch your tone. A broken coffee machine is no laughing matter, especially for an Israeli. But I do get your point. Realize, though, that Jesus was making a blanket statement. He was not saying that every Christian must have a certain number of holes punched into their tribulation suffering card before they are ready for heaven. His point was that the disciples and the church in general should expect that pain and heartache are going to come their way because of their alignment with Him. We should be ready for trouble. And rather than receiving such with shame, we should accept it with pride, recognizing that we have the joy of enduring some of the anguish that our Savior felt as He died for our salvation.

As I mentioned at the beginning of this chapter, I want to arm you with the reasons that a pre-trib rapture best fits both Scripture and logic. The goal is for you to not only know what you believe, but why you believe it.

Pre-Trib Argument 1: God's Pattern Is to Remove the Righteous Before Wrath

A simple reading through Scripture will reveal that time after time, God has removed His people before unleashing His wrath upon a sinful world. It wasn't initially that way. After Adam and Eve's sin, the wicked were removed from the righteous. "[God] drove out the man; and He placed cherubim at the east of the garden of Eden, and a flaming sword which turned every way, to guard the way to the tree of life" (Genesis 3:24). The Garden of Eden was a holy place where God had walked, so sinful man got the boot.

But then, time passed, and evil spread over the world. God regretted making mankind and decided to pour out His wrath on sinful humanity. However, "Noah found grace in the eyes of the LORD" (Genesis 6:8). So, rather than destroying Noah with the unrighteous, God exempted the righteous from the imminent onset of His judgment.

> Then the LORD said to Noah, "Come into the ark, you and all your household, because I have seen that you are righteous before Me in this generation. You shall take with you seven each of every clean animal, a male and his female; two each of animals that are unclean, a male and his female; also seven each of birds of the air, male and female, to keep the species alive on the face of all the earth. For after seven more days I will cause it to rain on the earth forty days and forty nights, and I will destroy from the face of the earth all living things that I have made" (7:1-4).

This same godly attribute was displayed toward Abraham's nephew, Lot. Sodom and Gomorrah were such cesspools of sin that God decided that it was time to let loose His judgment upon the cities. The Lord visited His servant, Abraham, and revealed to the patriarch His plan of destruction. Abraham, knowing that his nephew Lot lived in the region, began to bargain with God in typical Jewish fashion:

> Abraham came near [to God] and said, "Would You also destroy the righteous with the wicked? Suppose there were fifty righteous within the city; would You also destroy the place and not spare it for the fifty righteous that were in it? Far be it from You to do such a thing as this, to slay the righteous with the wicked, so that the righteous should be as the wicked; far be it from You! Shall not the Judge of all the earth do right?" So the LORD said, "If I find in Sodom fifty righteous within the city, then I will spare all the place for their sakes" (Genesis 18:23-28).

Abraham then decreased the number to 45, then to 40. Five times, Abraham sought to renegotiate the deal, bringing the number all the way down to 10. But the numbers are not what is important. Abraham understood that it was not in God's character to subject the righteous to His intentional wrath against the unrighteous. Ultimately, the cities of Sodom and Gomorrah were destroyed, but not before God rescued righteous Lot and his family from His judgment.

Christians are told to separate themselves from the world. John wrote in his first letter, "Do not love the world or the things in the world" (1 John 2:15). But this was a spiritual separation he was speaking of. We cannot physically separate ourselves from the world. Yes, we can buy land in Montana, build a compound, and hide behind electric fences topped with razor wire. However, if God's judgment comes, all your defenses won't be able to stop it. Only God has the ability to separate His church from the discipline He is bringing upon Israel and wrath He is pouring out upon the sinful world. What a comfort it is to know that removing His bride from the coming onslaught is exactly what He has promised to do.

Pre-Trib Argument 2: Christ's Return Is Imminent

As Jesus was closing the canon of Scripture, He emphasized His imminent return. "Behold, I am coming quickly! Blessed is he who keeps the words of the prophecy of this book…And behold, I am coming quickly, and My reward is with Me, to give to every one according to his work" (Revelation 22:7, 12). Merriam-Webster defines the word *imminent* as "ready to take place" and "happening soon."[13] When it comes to Bible prophecy, it is the latter definition that most people seem to focus on. "If Jesus' return was imminent in the first century, it should have happened soon after He promised to come quickly—or at least at some point in the last 2,000 years!"

But biblical imminence has more to do with the first definition—that it is "ready to take place." When Jesus said He was coming quickly, He was letting His readers know that all is ready and He could come at any moment. That is why Paul was convinced that Jesus could come in his lifetime. Notice that he used the pronoun *we* throughout this all-important passage:

> This we say to you by the word of the Lord, that we who are alive and remain until the coming of the Lord will by no means precede those who are asleep. For the Lord Himself will descend from heaven with a shout, with the voice of an archangel, and with the trumpet of God. And the dead in Christ will rise first. Then we who are alive and remain shall be caught up together with them in the clouds to meet the Lord in the air. And thus we shall

always be with the Lord. Therefore comfort one another
with these words (1 Thessalonians 4:15-18).

Paul was ready and waiting. He had been transported once up to
heaven (2 Corinthians 12:1-4), and he was more than ready to take a
return flight. In both Jesus' and Paul's words, there are no qualifying
events that must take place before Christ's return. There is a window
of time that Paul creates with the following words of 2 Thessalonians
2, which firmly sets borders between which the rapture must occur:

> The mystery of lawlessness is already at work; only He who
> now restrains will do so until He is taken out of the way.
> And then the lawless one will be revealed, whom the Lord
> will consume with the breath of His mouth and destroy
> with the brightness of His coming (vv. 7-8).

The opening of this window is the moment of Paul's writing.
Because of his sense of imminency, the rapture could have happened
anytime after those words were written. The closing of the window
is the removal of the Restrainer. Paul's temporal phrase "and then,"
which introduces the rise of the antichrist, necessitates that the rapture must have already happened. If the antichrist is on the scene,
the church is not.

Even in the Olivet Discourse, the "beginning of sorrows" just tells
us what the world will be like in the last days (Matthew 24:8). Any
specific events mentioned will pertain to the tribulation, not the rapture. And there is certainly no place in Scripture that says, "Once you
see the rise of the antichrist, then begin to count out three-and-a-half
years. Then Jesus will come in the clouds to take you." Or, "When
the third temple is built, understand that there will be only seven
years of horror and misery before Jesus will come again to take the
church to be with Him."

All is ready. At any moment, Jesus can come to take us to be with Him. In the meantime, keep one eye on the mission field around you and one eye on the clouds above; keep one hand on the plow and one hand lifted in praise to Him.

Pre-Trib Argument 3: The Son's Work Is Sufficient for the Father

Think back to when our Savior was suffering on the cross. He had been beaten and tortured. He had been mocked and spat upon. Finally, He had been nailed to a wooden crossbar and hung up to slowly suffocate to death. John described the final moments before Jesus died:

> After this, Jesus, knowing that all things were now accomplished, that the Scripture might be fulfilled, said, "I thirst!" Now a vessel full of sour wine was sitting there; and they filled a sponge with sour wine, put it on hyssop, and put it to His mouth. So when Jesus had received the sour wine, He said, "It is finished!" And bowing His head, He gave up His spirit (John 19:28-30).

Look again at those final words: "It is finished!" The penalty for our sins was paid. The door was opened for our righteousness. Reconciliation with our Creator was at hand. We now have the freedom to "come boldly to the throne of grace, that we may obtain mercy and find grace to help in time of need" (Hebrews 4:16). While on the cross, Jesus didn't cry out, "It is mostly finished!" John included no asterisk leading to a footnote that said, "Author's note: Jesus meant 'finished-ish.' You're still going to need a little fire in your life to make you truly righteous."

The work of our Messiah on the cross was wholly sufficient for our justification. There is no more penalty left to be paid. As the great nineteenth-century hymn goes:

Jesus paid it all,
All to Him I owe;
Sin had left a crimson stain,
He washed it white as snow.

Pre-Trib Argument 4: A Literal Interpretation of Scripture

Any rapture view other than the pre-trib view must take either part or all of Revelation 4–18 and look for the church somewhere in the events. Unfortunately for them, it will be a futile search. Some will say, "But Amir, you are making an argument from silence. Just because the church is not mentioned doesn't mean it isn't there." That reasoning falls apart, however, with the context. Chapters 1–3 focus exclusively on the church. To say that, as Revelation continues, the church is enduring the suffering of the judgments but John just neglects to mention them is illogical and ridiculous. If the Lamb is responsible for opening the seals that unleash havoc and plagues on His beloved bride, how does He not even acknowledge her? The only way to place the church into the judgments of Revelation is to allegorize the events.

The same holds true for Jesus' words in the Olivet Discourse in Matthew 24–25 and Paul's encouragements to the church in 1 Corinthians 15, 1 Thessalonians 4 and 5, and 2 Thessalonians 2. The only conclusion derived from a literal interpretation of these chapters is that Jesus can come at any moment to take His church to be with Him. We will look more at the importance of a literal hermeneutic in the next chapter.

Pre-Trib Argument 5: The Twofold Purpose of the Tribulation

The tribulation is the time of Jacob's trouble and the day of God's wrath upon the unbelieving world. It is discipline for the rebellious Jew and punishment for the sinful Gentile. As we saw in the last chapter, there is no place for the church in the tribulation. The only purpose one can come up with is that Jesus as the Groom wants a holier, more righteous bride, so He is going to purify her by fire. But if we have been made perfectly clean by the blood of our Messiah, what will suffering do for us? How do you improve on the perfection imputed to us by the act of a perfect Savior?

God has planned the tribulation for a reason. The church is not part of that reason.

Pre-Trib Argument 6: A True Comfort

As we saw in pre-trib argument 2, Paul wrote to the Thessalonians about the coming rapture. At the end of that passage, he concluded by saying, "Therefore comfort one another with these words" (1 Thessalonians 4:18). He then went on in chapter 5 to talk about the suddenness of Christ's return and the necessity of the church remaining vigilant in carrying out its mission in a darkened world. He wrapped up the section by writing,

> God did not appoint us to wrath, but to obtain salvation through our Lord Jesus Christ, who died for us, that whether we wake or sleep, we should live together with Him. Therefore comfort each other and edify one another, just as you also are doing (5:9-11).

My friend, we are not appointed to wrath. As the church, there "is therefore now no condemnation to those who are in Christ Jesus, who do not walk according to the flesh, but according to the Spirit" (Romans 8:1). Yes, we will have tribulations—some more than others. But for those who are in Christ Jesus, we will not have *the* tribulation. Jesus is coming to remove the church, His bride, before the judgment begins.

No, the tribulation has not begun. If Jesus is your Savior and your Lord, you will be raptured before it starts. I pray that you are comforted with those words.

SAVE THE DATE

In this world, there are great pairings. Some are historical. How can you have Samson without Delilah, or Marc Antony without Cleopatra? In the entertainment world, where would Lucy be without Desi or Snoopy without Woodstock? And in the culinary realm, peas just aren't the same without carrots. And who would want hummus without pita or pork chops without applesauce? Now, as a Jew, I would never eat pork chops—that is, unless they were richly seasoned and grilled to a perfect medium well.

When it comes to the end times, there are also significant pairings. We find the beast and his evil partner, the false prophet. Testifying in Jerusalem, we have the witness and...well...the second witness. And linked forever in God's timeline, you cannot have the tribulation without the rapture. If you ask why the two must be together, then let me invite you to reread the previous chapter. The church cannot and will not be on this earth when God's wrath strikes. That is not how our loving Father operates, and the church is not the group for whom the tribulation was designed. For the tribulation to happen, the rapture must come first.

Has the tribulation begun? If you have received Jesus as your Lord and Savior and you are reading this from a location somewhere on the surface of the earth, then the answer is quite obviously no. I guess you could be reading this in an airplane or on the space station, and the answer would still be no.

A reason why this link between a pre-tribulational rapture and the tribulation may feel so important is that it seems that if we can find the timing to the one, then we can reasonably surmise the timing for the other. Have you figured out the date for the rapture? Then you know the tribulation is coming soon after. Have you calculated when the tribulation will begin? Then you can be sure that the rapture will take place not long before.

Normally, logic like this would have biblical detectives excited because it would mean that the secret to one of the great mysteries of Christendom might soon be revealed. But it is Jesus Himself who throws a damper on any enthusiasm over pinpointing a date for meeting Him in the clouds. On the Mount of Olives, He told His disciples, "Of that day and hour no one knows, not even the angels of heaven, but My Father only" (Matthew 24:36). Essentially, Jesus said to His followers, "Listen, I can tell you all you want to know about the end times. But as for the timing of the rapture? No can do."

Why is the Father so secretive when it comes to His Son's return? Because He knows us. Jesus described it this way in the same conversation on the Mount of Olives:

> Watch therefore, for you do not know what hour your Lord is coming. But know this, that if the master of the house had known what hour the thief would come, he would have watched and not allowed his house to be broken into. Therefore you also be ready, for the Son of Man is coming at an hour you do not expect (vv. 42-44).

If you know that on Wednesday at 10:00 p.m. a thief is going to break into your house but that you are safe until then, then it is likely that Sunday, Monday, and Tuesday you'll just go about your daily business. No need to worry about anybody stealing anything because you've already got a Save-the-Date from your local burglar. You'll probably even leave your doors unlocked and your windows open to let in the breeze, all the way up till Wednesday at 9:00 p.m. Only then will you get your weapons ready and predial your phone with the police emergency number.

That is exactly how most Christians would live their lives if they knew when Jesus was returning. "I'm just going to do my thing up until Wednesday at 9:00 p.m. Then I'll do some quick repenting, call my neighbors to read *The Four Spiritual Laws* to them so I can say I've been a witness, give an online donation of all my savings to my church to catch up for all those missed tithes, then wait to rocket up to my Lord!" God knows us too well. He understands that we can't be trusted with that much knowledge. Humanity works best with a little mystery, and the timing of Jesus' return for the church is exactly the kind of mystery we need.

Does this mean that we have no clue as to when the rapture will happen? Look again at Jesus' words. He said, "Of that day and hour no one knows." We'll never pinpoint the precise moment of Jesus' return for His church. But the Bible does give us tools so that we can determine the likely time frame. Like any to-do project we have to accomplish around the house, having the right tool makes all the difference so that you're not stuck trying to pound in a nail with the handle of a screwdriver. When we open our little red toolbox to begin our rapture timing DIY project, we'll find in there five tools perfectly designed for the task at hand.

WHEN IS THE SEASON?

Timing Tool 1: Bible Prophecy

God filled nearly a third of the Bible with talk of future events because He wants you to know His plans. As He declared through the prophet Isaiah,

> Remember the former things of old,
> for I am God, and there is no other;
> I am God, and there is none like Me,
> declaring the end from the beginning,
> And from ancient times things that are not yet done,
> saying, "My counsel shall stand,
> and I will do all My pleasure" (Isaiah 46:9-10).

God creates His plans, and then He tells the world about those plans. It used to be that He declared "the end from the beginning" through His prophets. But now we have His full counsel in the Scriptures. How do we know that the Bible contains all that God intended for us to know about the future? Because the Holy Spirit superintended its creation. Peter wrote, "No prophecy of Scripture is of any private interpretation, for prophecy never came by the will of man, but holy men of God spoke as they were moved by the Holy Spirit" (2 Peter 1:20-21).

When we look for God's premeditated actions and the timing of those actions, we are not just grasping at random straws, trying to determine omens or read the tea leaves. God has filled the Bible with His timeline stretching from the very beginning to today and all the way to the end times. Our job is to take those passages that look to future events and interpret them in a way that seeks the author's original intent. Unfortunately, there is so much shoddy interpretation that takes passages of Scripture and asks, "How can I make this author's words fit my doctrine?" Faithful interpretation asks, "How must I adapt my doctrine to fit this author's words?"

That means looking at the passages in a literal manner, unless they clearly should be taken otherwise. When Jesus spoke in parables, His audience knew that the stories were not a retelling of actual historical events. They were illustrations of important spiritual truths, and they should be construed as such. However, the normal, go-to way to interpret Scripture is to expect that the author intended his words to be understood exactly as he wrote them. Trustworthy doctrine is built on "This is what he wrote" instead of "This is what he really meant."

Good interpretation also means looking at these prophetic passages in the context of the rest of the Bible. Paul wrote to Timothy, "All Scripture is given by inspiration of God" (2 Timothy 3:16). If it all comes from a perfect God, then we know that it will never contradict itself. So, if we come up with an interpretation of a prophecy that is contrary to another passage in the Bible, then we know that the fault is not with God but with our own conclusions. This gives us wonderful checks and balances when it comes to analyzing not just prophecy but all of Scripture.

If we want to understand God's plans for the end times, including the time frame of the rapture and tribulation, Bible prophecy is the first and best place for us to start. Without this tool, we are attempting to understand God's infinite wisdom with nothing but our pitifully finite minds. In the next chapter, we will primarily use this essential timing tool, along with timing tool 2, to see how close we might be to the rapture and the tribulation.

Timing Tool 2: Current Events

The rapture can take place at any moment. There is nothing else that needs to be done, no other event that must take place. That is why Paul was convinced that he and those around him might experience this glorious event. As we saw earlier, he used the first-person plural when he talked about the rapture: "Then we who are alive and remain shall be caught up together with them in the clouds to meet the Lord in the air. And thus we shall always be with the Lord" (1 Thessalonians 4:17). He didn't say, "Then they—those Christians in the future, like maybe 2,000 years from now—who are alive…" Paul was fully expecting that he could be snatched up at any time, and he was excited for it to happen.

What we see in current events around us are clues that indicate the onset of the tribulation. And if the tribulation is close, then we know that the rapture is closer. Going back to Jesus' conversation with the disciples on the Mount of Olives, it all began with them asking specifically about the timing of the "end of the age" (Matthew 24:3). Jesus responded:

> Take heed that no one deceives you. For many will come in My name, saying, "I am the Christ," and will deceive many. And you will hear of wars and rumors of wars. See that you are not troubled; for all these things must come to pass, but the end is not yet. For nation will rise against nation, and kingdom against kingdom. And there will be famines, pestilences, and earthquakes in various places. All these are the beginning of sorrows (vv. 4-8).

I can't tell you what the world will be like at the time you read this book. Events are moving much too quickly, and I am no prophet. I can only tell you what I see now, and it's certainly crazy enough to fit the bill for what Jesus prophesied. Again, in the next chapter, we will look with more detail at what Jesus predicted and in what ways our world matches His words.

Just a quick preview for you, though. Everything that we see taking place in the world around us points to the rapture/tribulation time frame. But remember, we are not currently in the tribulation. Jesus said in Matthew 24 that this is all "the beginning of sorrows" (v. 8). In the Greek text, the phrase translated "sorrows" speaks of "birth pangs." Although many of the leading minds of our great medical community have now determined that it is somehow possible for men to have babies, I, for one, have not given birth. Nor do I want to. Nor could I, despite what the fools of this age have concluded. However, my wife has had four children, and I am so grateful to her for being the bearer of our brood. One truth that I have learned from her is that a birth pang can be very painful, but it is nothing compared to the actual birth. What we are experiencing now in this messy world is nothing compared to what is coming during the tribulation.

Does this frighten you? If you are a follower of Jesus Christ, it shouldn't. Once again, look at Jesus' words to His disciples: "See that you are not troubled; for all these things must come to pass, but the end is not yet" (Matthew 24:6). Don't be afraid. Like the birth pangs signal a soon-coming birth, so these events of trial and tribulation signal the soon-coming seven-year tribulation of God's wrath. And they also let us know that the time is even sooner for the church's departure from this world.

Timing Tool 3: God and Israel

My grandparents on my mother's side were from Poland. If you had asked them to come settle in Mandatory Palestine, the internationally accepted name of the area of Israel through much of the first half of the twentieth century, they would have laughed at you. Why would they possibly want to leave what they had? Europe was much better. They flourished there. Israel was just deserts and swamps. Not enough water or too much water; poisonous snakes or malarial mosquitos. Come and work a kibbutz! Work hard, live miserably, die young!

Ultimately, it wasn't their wills that mattered. It was God's plan. The Lord had made a promise with the Israelites as they were preparing to enter the land. Through Moses, He said,

> Now it shall come to pass, when all these things come upon you, the blessing and the curse which I have set before you, and you call them to mind among all the nations where the LORD your God drives you, and you return to the LORD your God and obey His voice, according to all that I command you today, you and your children, with all

your heart and with all your soul, that the LORD your God will bring you back from captivity, and have compassion on you, and gather you again from all the nations where the LORD your God has scattered you. If any of you are driven out to the farthest parts under heaven, from there the LORD your God will gather you, and from there He will bring you. Then the LORD your God will bring you to the land which your fathers possessed, and you shall possess it. He will prosper you and multiply you more than your fathers. And the LORD your God will circumcise your heart and the heart of your descendants, to love the LORD your God with all your heart and with all your soul, that you may live (Deuteronomy 30:1-6).

Many say that this was fulfilled after the Jewish exile to Babylon. But how could that be possible? When was post-exilic Israel, even up through the time of Jesus, more prosperous than the time of King David or King Solomon? When has the whole nation of Israel loved the Lord with their whole hearts and their entire souls? Even up to today, this remains unfulfilled. Certainly, Jews have been gathered from the "farthest parts under heaven." However, it will not be until after the tribulation that the repentant circumcision of the heart will take place throughout the nation.

Using the reestablishment of the nation of Israel as a bellwether, God has set the stage for His end-times scenario. It's hard to imagine now, but the State of Israel's existence would have been folly to my grandparents, as it was to the rest of the world's population prior to 1948. Most of this generation misses this point because we live in a world where Israel is an accepted entity. However, for almost 2,000 years prior to this generation, the idea of an Israeli state would have been ludicrous.

But God knew. He planned. He promised:

Who has heard such a thing?
Who has seen such things?
Shall the earth be made to give birth in one day?
Or shall a nation be born at once?
For as soon as Zion was in labor,
she gave birth to her children (Isaiah 66:8).

It is this generation that saw the fulfillment of Isaiah's prophecy. How can a nation be born overnight? May 14, 1948, was a hectic day for the Zionist cause. The British Mandate was ending the next day, and Israel's leaders had been scrambling to finalize the wording for the nation's Declaration of Independence. By the time a vote was passed on the document, only an hour remained before the scheduled signing ceremony at the Tel Aviv Museum—not enough time for the final draft to be fully prepared for signatures. So the signatures were collected on a piece of paper, and that paper was later sewn on to the actual Declaration! As Isaiah wrote, "Who has heard such a thing?" On May 13, 1948, there was no country called Israel. On May 14, 1948, the State of Israel had been born. A nation born in a day!

How close is the tribulation? An Israeli state is necessary for the events of the tribulation to occur. For 2,000 years, there was no Israeli state. Now, there is not only an Israeli state, but it is thriving. In fact, it is becoming so wealthy that it is attracting the attention of economically struggling countries with large militaries and morally and spiritually compromised leadership, such as the ones spoken of in Ezekiel 38:2-6. Again, how close is the tribulation? Much closer than it has ever been before.

Timing Tool 4: Ezekiel 36–39

Much of what we know about the tribulation comes from the Old Testament. The second half of Daniel gives much insight into the coming antichrist. In the prophet's vision of the 70 weeks, he wrote:

> After the sixty-two weeks
> Messiah shall be cut off, but not for Himself;
> and the people of the prince who is to come
> shall destroy the city and the sanctuary.
> The end of it shall be with a flood,
> and till the end of the war desolations are determined.
>
> Then he shall confirm a covenant with many for one week;
> but in the middle of the week
> he shall bring an end to sacrifice and offering.
> And on the wing of abominations shall be one
>   who makes desolate,
> even until the consummation, which is determined,
> is poured out on the desolate (Daniel 9:26-27).

This puppet of Satan will arise and make a covenant of peace with Israel, which will last for three-and-a-half years. But after that time, he will betray the Jews and bring a fierce persecution upon them:

> He shall speak pompous words against the Most High,
> shall persecute the saints of the Most High,
> and shall intend to change times and law.
> Then the saints shall be given into his hand
> for a time and times and half a time (Daniel 7:25).

But the Old Testament prophet who tells us the most about the timing of the tribulation is Ezekiel. We've touched on much of this already, so I won't go into detail. But it is in Ezekiel 36 that we find a promise for the healing of the land. If you do an internet search for "Pictures of Israel prior to 1948," you will discover many interesting historical sights. What you will find very few of, however, are photographs of green landscapes. You will not see agriculture spread throughout the Jezreel Valley. You will not find thousands of fruit groves scattered from Dan to Eilat filled with an incredible bounty. Now search for "Images of Israel agriculture." What will appear on your computer screen is Bible prophecy fulfilled in your generation.

A revitalized land is nothing, however, without a revitalized people. In a valley filled with dry bones, Ezekiel watched as God first knit the bones together, then covered them with muscle and flesh, and finally breathed life into them. Then the Lord said to the prophet:

> Son of man, these bones are the whole house of Israel. They indeed say, "Our bones are dry, our hope is lost, and we ourselves are cut off!" Therefore prophesy and say to them, "Thus says the Lord GOD: 'Behold, O My people, I will open your graves and cause you to come up from your graves, and bring you into the land of Israel. Then you shall know that I am the LORD, when I have opened your graves, O My people, and brought you up from your graves. I will put My Spirit in you, and you shall live, and I will place you in your own land. Then you shall know that I, the LORD, have spoken it and performed it,' says the LORD" (Ezekiel 37:11-14).

Notice the location to which God says He will bring the people. Is it Eastern Europe? Maybe New York City or Southern California? Or what about Palestine or the British Mandate? No, He said that He would bring them "into the land of Israel...I will place you in your own land." One cannot place someone in the land of Israel if there is no land of Israel. So, God reestablished the Jewish Holy Land— the land of His promise. God said it; God did it. "Here's your land; now come on home."

Those two chapters are the happy side of the Ezekiel prophecy. The downside is found in chapters 38–39. There, we see nations coming against Israel seeking to plunder and destroy. It would be quite difficult to plunder and destroy a nation that doesn't exist. For centuries, a missing Israel led to all sorts of allegorical and justifying interpretations searching for "what Ezekiel *really* meant." But then in May 1948, God said, "No, if only you had been patient and trusted Me to put all the pieces together, you would have seen that what I said through Ezekiel was really quite simple and straightforward. This coalition of countries will attack My people exactly like I said. And now, may I present to you Israel!"

No State of Israel? No tribulation. A thriving State of Israel? Better look to the skies.

Timing Tool 5: The Parable of the Fig Tree

What generation are you? It seems culture is obsessed with generations. Are you a Boomer or a Buster? Maybe you're a Millennial or even a Gen Z. Or maybe you are part of the Greatest Generation, that hard-working, self-sacrificing group of men and women born during the first quarter of the twentieth century. Whatever the category to which your birth year may designate you, there is one unifying generation for all of us. Every one of us is part of the Fig Tree Generation.

In the Olivet Discourse that we've referred to so often in this chapter, there is an unusual break in the style of Jesus' teaching. In the middle of teaching prophetic narrative, our Lord cuts out for a parable:

> Now learn this parable from the fig tree: When its branch has already become tender and puts forth leaves, you know that summer is near. So you also, when you see all these things, know that it is near—at the doors! Assuredly, I say to you, this generation will by no means pass away till all these things take place. Heaven and earth will pass away, but My words will by no means pass away (Matthew 24:32-35).

Remember what a parable is: It's a story that illustrates a greater truth. The wording here is short and precise. The meaning is simple to discern. When you see signs indicating the approach of an event, then expect to soon witness the occasion. Fig trees sprout in the spring, which means that summer is right around the corner.

Jesus told the disciples that the signs that He had just spoken of to them would be followed by the tribulation and the end of all things. It is just as natural as summer following the budding of the plants in spring. See leaves? Summer is near. See these signs? The end is near.

But there is another layer to this seemingly simple parable, and it is found in the symbolism of the fig tree. "Now hold on, Amir! Who are you to determine when you have to interpret literally and when you get to look for symbolism?" Understandable question. However, I'm not determining it. Jesus did. He called this the *parable* of the fig tree. The Bible is so clear when we just slow down and look at what the words say.

The Bible often employs what is called symbolism. With symbolism, people and events will represent something greater than themselves. The rainbow represents the end of a storm, as well as God's covenant with the world to never again destroy it with water. The dove can merely be a bird, or it can represent the Holy Spirit. The Passover Lamb reminded the Jews of God rescuing them from Egyptian slavery, while also representing Jesus' sacrifice on the cross for the sins of the whole world. And fig trees can be a food-producing plant, while also representing the nation of Israel. The prophet Hosea wrote:

> I found Israel
> like grapes in the wilderness;
> I saw your fathers
> as the firstfruits on the fig tree in its first season (9:10).

In the Scriptures we see several agricultural symbols used to communicate various aspects of Israel. The vine represents the spiritual privileges of Israel, which the church can be grafted into. Closeness with God does not just belong to the Jews but is offered to all. Jesus, as the true Vine, said, "I am the vine, you are the branches. He who abides in Me, and I in him, bears much fruit; for without Me you can do nothing" (John 15:5).

The olive tree represents the religious privilege of the Jews as priests and servants of the most high God. Yet these roles, too, are opened to the church as priests of the new covenant under Jesus Christ:

> You are a chosen generation, a royal priesthood, a holy nation, His own special people, that you may proclaim the praises of Him who called you out of darkness into His marvelous light; who once were not a people but are now the people of God, who had not obtained mercy but now have obtained mercy (1 Peter 2:9-10).

With these new honors of servanthood, however, the church must ensure it never forgets who had the roles first.

> If some of the branches were broken off, and you, being a wild olive tree, were grafted in among them, and with them became a partaker of the root and fatness of the olive tree, do not boast against the branches. But if you do boast, remember that you do not support the root, but the root supports you (Romans 11:17-18).

The one agricultural symbol of Israel that is never opened to the church is that of the fig tree. Never in Scripture will you find the church connected with that representation. The fig tree signifies the national privileges of Israel, which belong to the Jews alone. Christians have the privilege of being part of the vine and the olive tree; they have the privilege of witnessing God's work with the fig tree.

So, what is this parable telling us? When you see the fig tree budding and pushing forth leaves, know that the end is coming. The fig tree is Israel, and Israel has more than budded. It has pushed out its leaves and is now producing massive amounts of fruit. And what was Jesus' ultimate point? The generation that sees this miraculous sign of the fig tree will not pass away until "all these things take place" (Matthew 24:34).

Who is this generation? If you have a smartphone, take it out, open your camera app, set it to selfie mode, and snap a picture. See that face? That person is part of the generation that will not pass away until the return of Christ. Yes, it includes you!

Don't get the wrong idea. If you decide to jump out of an airplane without a parachute, you will most certainly pass away. It is this *collective* generation that will not die. There are people alive today who will be among those taken up in the rapture to meet Jesus in the clouds. If it happens soon, it will be most of us. If the Lord tarries, it will only be some. But it is this generation that will see Jesus return to receive His church unto Himself.

WHEN IS THE DATE?

So, when will the rapture and the tribulation take place?

I have no idea.

But before you get exasperated and toss this book into your energy-efficient pellet stove, I can still help you out a little. I can tell you with certainty when the rapture will *not* happen.

First, it will not happen when you think it will happen. If you've listened to all your online teachers and read all your secret Bible code books, if you've calculated the years and weeks and days then compared them to all the Old Covenant feasts, and you've put in hour upon hour and have finally come up with the day when the rapture absolutely 100 percent will happen, then congratulations! You have discovered the one day on which the rapture is certain not to take place. Jesus said that no one knows. You are a "no one."

Second, it will not happen when your pastor, online preacher, or that guy with the new book says it is going to happen. I don't care if they understand ancient numerology. It makes no difference if they can read Hebrew backwards, sideways, or in spirals. It doesn't matter the algorithms they have created, the links they've discovered to Hammurabi's Code, or their interpretation of the lost creation myth written on the red marble pyramid left on their porch by a space alien. No matter what tool they are using or special insight they claim to have acquired, they are without a doubt completely wrong. Every Bible teacher, including me, is also a "no one."

Don't get caught up in the date trap. Forget the speculation. Run away from those with special insight or prophetic words regarding signs and moons and hidden meanings. God gave us a Bible that is written at a level that most of us can understand clearly. You don't need anyone to tell you about the words behind the words.

Besides, our focus should be less on when it will happen than on the truth that it will happen. And based on the tools we have employed, we know that it will happen soon. What does *soon* mean? It could mean hours, days, months, or years. What I can encourage you with is that we are the first people in the history of the church who can truly say that it will not happen generations from now. Never before has soon been so soon. So, be encouraged. While we can't know the exact date, it is undoubtedly around the corner.

EVERYWHERE A SIGN

While the *when* of the end times may not be on the same level of importance as how we serve the Lord in the short window of time that exists, it is still significant. Otherwise, when Jesus' disciples came to Him on the Mount of Olives and asked, "Tell us, when will these things be? And what will be the sign of Your coming, and of the end of the age?" (Matthew 24:3), He would have responded, "Don't worry about it. Just keep doing the things I've told you to do."

Instead, if you'll recall, Jesus answered,

> Take heed that no one deceives you. For many will come in My name, saying, "I am the Christ," and will deceive many. And you will hear of wars and rumors of wars. See that you are not troubled; for all these things must come to pass, but the end is not yet. For nation will rise against nation, and kingdom against kingdom. And there will be famines, pestilences, and earthquakes in various places. All these are the beginning of sorrows (Matthew 24:4-8).

Jesus placed the coming tribulation into a future setting, saying, "This is what the world will look like prior to the coming wrath." It is only after He established the global backdrop that He transitioned to the actual events of the tribulation by using the temporal word "then": "Then they will deliver you up to tribulation and kill you, and you will be hated by all nations for My name's sake" (v. 9).

First this, then that. First the beginning of sorrows, then the wrath.

Why did Jesus feel it necessary to include timing clues? Because it is vital information. As we've already seen, God wants us to know His plans, so He has given us a book packed cover to cover with essential information. Recognizing God's handiwork in the world around us and seeing how it fits into His end-times plans gives us much more insight into who He is and how He operates. It also lets us know how we fit into His purposes.

Knowing the timing also provides motivation, and that is my primary purpose for this chapter. As we look through the signs of the end times, both the birth pangs and the global preparations, we will see just how close we are to our time running out on this earth. My prayer is that one of two actions will take place in your heart as a result. If you are not a Christian, I hope that you will be motivated to give your life to Christ now while there is still time. As we'll see in the following two chapters, this earth is not where you want to be when God pours out His wrath. If you are a Christian, I trust that when you see how the stage is set for the Lord's return, that your love for those around you will kick into high gear, moving you to share the truth with them so that they, too, can be rescued from the tribulation that is soon to come.

THE SIGNS OF THE TIMES

Attempting to communicate the current world condition in book format is a near-impossible task, particularly in today's geopolitical climate. It is like a father taking his son to the racetrack so he can show him his favorite driver. No sooner does he point out the correct car than it speeds past and is gone. For most publishing houses, it is a full year from the moment an author turns in a manuscript to the time the book hits the shelves. Even with my publisher, Harvest House, who always seems to find ways to work miracles, it is still a minimum of six months lag time.

Still, it is important that we take a snapshot of the world so we can compare it to the signs of the times that the Bible has laid out. What follows is a picture of our world as I'm writing this, understanding that by the time you read this book our global situation may be similar or very different. No matter what may transpire between now and then, there is little doubt that these are the beginning of sorrows.

Sign 1: Wars and Rumors of Wars

The war between Russia and Ukraine rages, and the great bear of Eurasia continues to hold the upper hand. Europe has imposed its sanctions and hurled its threats, but Russian president Vladimir Putin knows he has the EU in a headlock. What is giving him the power? Energy! Europe allowed itself to become dependent upon Russian gas, and Moscow is shutting down the supply. "You're weaponizing your energy," the Europeans complain, to which Putin replies, "Da, and…?"

Then, suddenly, the two underwater gas pipelines of Nord Stream 1 and Nord Stream 2 exploded deep in the Baltic Sea. Even though the second pipeline had never come online, it was still there as a backup. But now both are gone, and Europe's energy woes have become even greater. Where are they looking for help? Israel, with its massive gas fields. If Israel takes away Russia's power over Europe by supplying the continent's gas, that will be a situation that Putin and his government cannot tolerate.

But it's not just in the Baltic region that this particular birth pang is felt. No matter where you live, you don't have to look far to find wars and rumors of wars. In Africa, there is cross-border fighting between Ethiopia and Sudan, and there are internal hostilities in Somalia, Nigeria, the Democratic Republic of the Congo, the

Central African Republic, Mali, Chad, and others. Blood continues to be shed in Asian countries such as Afghanistan and Myanmar, and there is the great "rumor of war" that China continually stokes as they encircle Taiwan on the seas and fly into the island nation's airspace. The Middle East is a hotbed of conflict. Lives are being lost in Syria, Iraq, Iran, Lebanon, Yemen, Saudi Arabia, Israel, Gaza, and the West Bank. For those of you in the US, you just need to look south to the Mexican drug war that is taking thousands of lives and is spreading across your border.

Through all this international mayhem, alliances are being formed that fit like puzzle pieces into the Ezekiel 38 scenario. Iran's power is surging as Europe and the United States weakened their sanctions in an attempt to get a feckless new nuclear agreement signed. As time has gone by, the likelihood of signing an agreement has lessened. But even if a deal was reached, does anyone really think that Iran will halt its nuclear aspirations? Even the International Atomic Energy Agency (IAEA), an autonomous United Nations organization that seems to do all it can to paint Tehran in the rosiest of colors, was forced to admit that it was "not in a position to provide assurance that Iran's nuclear program is exclusively peaceful."[14] An admission like this from the IAEA is tantamount to them saying, "We can't be sure, but the Ayatollah just might have a stack of nukes hidden behind the boxes of old records in his basement."

Many have asked me whether I think that Iran would use a nuclear weapon against Israel. I don't, at least not in the traditional way of firing a missile at us. It is much more likely that they will arm one of their proxies with a small device or a dirty bomb that will then be smuggled in from Syria or Gaza and detonated in Tel Aviv. Iran has become the terrorist version of Fagin from *Oliver Twist*. The regime leaders send out all their little urchin proxy militias to do their terrorist work while they sit back safely in their palaces reaping the rewards.

Tehran would love to see Israel destroyed. But the regime doesn't want to be the one who starts the war. Their power is growing, but they are not nearly strong enough yet for that fight. Instead, they prefer for someone else to launch an attack, then they'll tag in. Isn't it convenient, then, that Iran is building a closer military and economic friendship with Russia, the Gog of Ezekiel 38? They are aiding one another with weapons, with Iran selling the Russians militarized drones, and Russia selling Iran Sukhoi Su-35 fighter jets.[15] Russia is also allowing Iranian forces to move onto their bases in Syria, as Moscow has been forced to gradually relocate their military from the Middle East to the Ukraine conflict. This draws Iran and their proxies closer and closer to the Syrian border with Israel.

Who else will join Russia and Iran in their unholy Ezekiel 38 alliance? Turkey. So, it is not surprising to see the ties that are growing between Putin and Turkey's president Recep Tayyip Erdogan. Turkey needs friends because its economy and currency are both in freefall, and the nation will soon have to find some way to boost its economy. Libya, too, shows up in Ezekiel's scenario, and currently that country is descending into chaos with a disputed government and people fleeing for safety. Who is there to be their close ally, coming alongside them in this difficult time? Turkey, having reestablished close ties back in 2019 after many years of hostility between the countries.[16] The necessary connections for the prophesied Ezekiel 38 war have been forged.

The question remains: Why would this alliance attack Israel as is foretold in Ezekiel 38? What is it that all these countries can find in my small nation? A whole lot of money and, as we just saw with Israel's offshore gas drilling, the potential to make a whole lot more. Remember, the Ezekiel 38 war is not about borders or religion or trying to help the Palestinians. It is all about plunder.

> Thus says the Lord GOD: "On that day it shall come to
> pass that thoughts will arise in your mind, and you will

make an evil plan: You will say, 'I will go up against a
land of unwalled villages; I will go to a peaceful people,
who dwell safely, all of them dwelling without walls, and
having neither bars nor gates'—to take plunder and to take
booty, to stretch out your hand against the waste places
that are again inhabited, and against a people gathered
from the nations, who have acquired livestock and goods,
who dwell in the midst of the land. Sheba, Dedan, the
merchants of Tarshish, and all their young lions will say to
you, 'Have you come to take plunder? Have you gathered
your army to take booty, to carry away silver and gold,
to take away livestock and goods, to take great plunder?'"
(Ezekiel 38:10-13).

Wars are being fought and many others are on the verge of breaking
out. Alliances are being formed that fit biblical prophecy. While there
may have been times in the past when more nations were involved
in actual fighting, never before have both the wars and the prophesied international alliances been extant at the same time.

Sign 2: Famines

This world was not created to experience disasters. In its original
form, tectonic plates did not shift, nor did massive storms take down
swaths of trees and cause widespread flooding. As we saw in an earlier
chapter, natural disasters are a part of the global decay that began as
a result of sin. With the progression of time bringing us near to the
beginning of the end, the devastating natural effects of death entering the world are greater than they've ever been. We should not be
surprised, though, because Jesus said to expect "famines, pestilences,
and earthquakes" (Matthew 24:7).

With all the progress that has been made in agricultural technology, it is amazing that famine is still so prevalent. But Jesus told

His disciples that desperate hunger would tragically continue. In January 2022, the World Food Programme identified South Sudan, Nigeria, Ethiopia, and Yemen as the locations with the most critical shortages of food. Other nations are feeling hunger due to climate issues. These countries include Afghanistan, Angola, Haiti, and Syria. Military conflicts are causing many to flee their homes and livelihoods, creating refugee-based food shortages in the Central African Republic, the Democratic Republic of the Congo, Myanmar, Somalia, Sudan, and the Central Sahel region, which includes Burkina Faso, Mali, and Niger.[17] Despotic regimes often control international aid, making it so that emergency supplies fail to reach the desperately hungry.

Sign 3: Pestilences

As far as diseases go, compared to where the world was the last two years, we are relatively pestilence-free. COVID is still around, but we are no longer in the middle of a global panic. There are still plenty of viruses lurking around, however, and I am fully expecting the next big pandemic to appear sooner rather than later.

My certainty that another world health crisis will soon confront us does not originate in a belief that deadly viruses are now rising up out of the ooze at a faster rate than normal. My conviction derives from the reality that many governments and world leaders have had a taste of pandemic power and they aren't ready to let it go. It is so much easier to impose one's will with an emergency health mandate as leverage. Close businesses, close schools, close churches. Limit movement, limit access, limit freedom. We'll tell you what you can do, when you can do it, and just who we will let you do it with. The past two years were a global case study of Lord Acton's observation, "Absolute power corrupts absolutely." I am confident that if an accommodating health crisis doesn't come along in the near future, the world's leadership won't hesitate to create one of their own. In fact, I've heard of a lab in Wuhan, China, that just might have a little experience at this.

Sign 4: Earthquakes

The number of earthquakes each year is increasing. Many different causes have been given for this upsurge. Some earthquakes are man-made due to mining, nuclear testing, fracking, pumping out liquid resources and gas, and nuclear testing. Others are purely natural, brought about by an increase in the shifting of tectonic plates or the release of underground energy caused by variations in the speed of the Earth's rotation.[18]

It is not just the frequency of earthquakes that is increasing, but also their intensity. The decade between 2004 and 2014 saw a 265 percent increase over the previous century of temblors greater than an 8.0 magnitude.[19] Experts say that Japan, New Zealand, and locations along the unstable Ring of Fire are all soon due for major shake-ups.[20] For those of you living on the west coast of the United States, your earthquake is coming soon. Many predict the Big One coming to California before 2030. Others say that the region that really needs to be worried is the Pacific Northwest. Called by *The New Yorker* "the worst natural disaster in the history of North America," the shifting of the tectonic plates in the Cascadia subduction zone could trigger an earthquake in the 8.0–9.2 range that could devastate everything from Seattle, Washington, all the way south to northern California.[21]

One more natural disaster not mentioned in the Olivet Discourse is the fires that are devastating forests, farmlands, and villages. Not long ago, Reuters reported one day's tally that included large wildfires in South Korea, Algeria, Morocco, Croatia, the Czech Republic, France, Germany, Greece, Italy, Portugal, Russia, Spain, Turkey, Canada, the US, and Argentina.[22] In many cases, it seems that what isn't burning is flooding. Recently, nearly one-third of Pakistan was under water, causing an estimated $30 billion of damage and leaving a humanitarian crisis of epic proportions.[23]

Sign 5: Globalism

The first four signs listed above covered the list that Jesus gave to the disciples in the Olivet Discourse. But as we expand our view to the rest of Scripture, there are other international transformations that must take place for the stage to be set for the beginning of the tribulation and the rise of the antichrist. All of them have to do with the breaking down of individualism and exceptionalism, both on a singular and national scale.

Global Government

When the antichrist ascends to his place of power, there will be a willingness by the people of many nations to discard their national loyalties and pledge their allegiances to this man. The fracturing of a citizen's ties to his country is a major mindset change that, barring some major national betrayal, doesn't happen overnight. Think about it: What would it take for you to say that you are no longer American or South African or British or Filipino? After a lifetime of living in my country and my years of military service, I can't imagine turning my back on being an Israeli. That sort of momentous change of perspective takes time and an intentional whittling away of national trust. That is the kind of shift that is being encouraged today.

Taking the place of patriotism and national pride is a sense that we are all one people. Forget borders and ethnic divides. We are all part of one race—the human race. There is certainly an upside to this mindset. Racism, whether personal or systemic, has no place in the world and especially in the church. The way that so many have used the Bible to elevate one race of people while denigrating another is a deplorable misuse of the Word of God.

"But wait, Amir! Aren't you always saying that God loves the Jews and has a special plan for the nation of Israel? Isn't that elevating a race of people? Doesn't that make you a racist?" Let me start from the last question and work my way back. No, it does not make me a racist. No, it is not elevating a race of people. And, yes, God does love the Jews and He most certainly has a special plan for them.

We are all servants of God and equal in His eyes. The Holy Spirit gifts one person one way and another person another way. Is one gift better than another? Not at all. In order to employ all the gifts needed for the good of everyone, the Holy Spirit calls one person to one ministry and another person to a different ministry. As Paul wrote:

> There are diversities of gifts, but the same Spirit. There are differences of ministries, but the same Lord. And there are diversities of activities, but it is the same God who works all in all. But the manifestation of the Spirit is given to each one for the profit of all (1 Corinthians 12:4-7).

All are gifted. All are called. All are equally loved and rank the same in the family of God. Am I specially blessed because of the ministry He has given to me? Ask me that question when I am saying goodbye to my family at the airport, knowing that I won't see them for the next four weeks.

Israel was called by God for a special task—to be His spokesnation to the world. Is it because He loved them more, or because there was something special about them? No. Just like with all gifts and callings, God simply made His choice. In Israel's case, He wanted a nation to reflect His glory. In His perfect wisdom He chose the Jews, despite knowing that they would utterly fail in their mission. Doesn't His faithfulness to the Jews encourage you knowing that despite your and my failings, God still loves us deeply and continues to allow us to serve Him?

While the spread of globalism may break down certain racial

divisions, it is the erosion of national borders that will have the greatest impact on the direction our world takes. The rule of the antichrist will see an international alliance similar to the European Union (EU), but on a global scale. Currently, the EU stretches over 4 million square kilometers (1.5 million square miles) and is populated by more than 447 million people.[24] Together, the member nations share a governing body, a court system, and a currency. The attitude within the EU of unity and assimilation is readily prepared for the rise of a singular leader. It is no wonder that the antichrist will quite probably come out of this alliance.

In Daniel's vision of the four beasts, the fourth and most vicious represents the Roman Empire, a power that overwhelmed the other nations of the world. Out of this beast will arise ten horns, which are ten kings. This is Europe, which has grown from what was the Western Roman Empire. From those ten horns will spring forth one more horn that will rule them all:

> I wished to know the truth about the fourth beast, which was different from all the others, exceedingly dreadful, with its teeth of iron and its nails of bronze, which devoured, broke in pieces, and trampled the residue with its feet; and the ten horns that were on its head, and the other horn which came up, before which three fell, namely, that horn which had eyes and a mouth which spoke pompous words, whose appearance was greater than his fellows. I was watching; and the same horn was making war against the saints, and prevailing against them, until the Ancient of Days came, and a judgment was made in favor of the saints of the Most High, and the time came for the saints to possess the kingdom (Daniel 7:19-22).

Many in America may say, "But is it really possible for this kind of international centralized rule to spread around the world, especially to us? We were built on individual freedom and exceptionalism." That is true. But look at how quickly your "individual freedom" collapsed when a pandemic swept through your nation. Now, picture this: a day comes when millions of your citizens suddenly disappear. Apart from the initial devastation deriving from the fiery aftermath of hundreds of thousands of driverless cars and numerous pilotless airplanes, the ensuing economic collapse will be unlike anything America has ever experienced. People will be looking for help, they will be looking for hope, and they will be looking for peace. If safety and stability in the face of that kind of horror means giving up some national sovereignty and a bit of personal freedom, that's a deal that even you, my dear friends in America, would have a hard time saying no to.

Global Economy

Never before have so many nations of the world been so open to homogenization. We've already mentioned the openness to global government demonstrated by the EU. There is also a spreading global economy in which the successes and failures of some nations have a huge impact on the economic stability of many others.

The EU is once again a perfect demonstration of this fact. As I write this, Russia continues to twist the energy garrote around Europe's throat, waiting for Europe to say "Uncle" and drop the sanctions. Russia's actions are not only causing gas shortages in the EU, but have led the OPEC+ nations to decrease their oil output in order to drive prices up. Who pays? All the nations of the world who depend upon these countries for their gas and oil. The energy shortage is greatly affecting the euro, dropping it below the US dollar to a 20-year low. While this may be a boon for American tourists traveling to Europe, it is a source of great concern for US companies that manufacture goods for European entities that may not be able to afford their products.[25]

The global economy can also be seen in the widespread increase of inflation. Pew Research analyzed the economies of 44 nations, and in 37 of those countries, the inflation rate for the first quarter of 2022 was at least double that of the first quarter of 2020. In 16 of those countries, it was greater than 4 times the earlier number. Although Israel's inflation rate is relatively low, it topped the list of rate changes in that period. Its rate of 3.36 percent is 25 times what it was previously.[26]

The global economy is not healthy, and when the church is removed, the bottom will fall out. The world will be ready for someone to step in and correct the international financial system. As for the individual, for a growing number of people, their personal banking is already done completely through a phone app. What will they care if their bank is local or an international entity? All they will want is stability, and that is something that the antichrist will readily provide.

Global Culture

I have spent the last decade and a half of my life traveling to wherever God calls me to teach His Word. I have been to more countries than I can count, and I have touched down on six of the seven continents. There are two constants that I see no matter where I go, from the richest countries to those struggling with great poverty: most of the houses have satellite dishes, and almost everyone has smartphones.

The world is smaller than it has ever been, and technology is the reason. Through television, the internet, and social media, the West has exported its culture across the globe. There may be a diversity in appearance and language from one person to another, but the music they listen to, the TikTok videos they watch, and the television series they follow are all the same. The world has shrunk to the size of a computer screen. A teen in Boise, Idaho, may log into a video game and find himself playing against a Millennial call-center employee in Bangalore, a 42-year-old bank employee in Davao, and an 8-year-old kid in Buenos Aires. And he won't even think twice about it because international connections are now the norm.

Not only is technology linking people across international lines, but it is also being used to break down the moral standards of many nations by presenting sin as normal. Television, movies, and social media are intentionally seeking to present as acceptable—and in many cases, laudable—homosexuality, transgenderism, abortion, sex outside of marriage, marijuana use, cohabitation, and any other vice you can think of. At the same time, these media are presenting anyone opposed to these activities as antiquated, bigoted, and hateful. It is at the point now that even speaking against what the Bible clearly communicates as sin can lead to verbal and physical attacks and a canceling from culture. The younger generation is being militarized, and the beginnings of this "freedom policing" can be seen in the violent acts of Antifa and other anarchist groups in many countries in the West.

It used to be that the "them against us" mindset was based on borders or political ideology. The Cold War and the post-9/11 war on terrorism united citizens within their countries who wanted to protect themselves against the evils from the outside. But now people are being told to look for their enemies in their cities and their neighborhoods and their families. The bad people are the ones who don't think as they do. The "us" reaches across international borders to anyone who agrees with their views of acceptance and inclusion. You can find the "them" among Christians and conservatives and other "bigoted" folk. When it is time for the antichrist to step forward, he will tap into the "us" mindset, and the people of the world will be ready to follow him lockstep.

Global Religion

When the antichrist ascends to his position, he will not just be a political leader, but a spiritual one. Not only will he unite people's minds, but he will draw in their hearts, their loyalty, and their adoration. This has led to speculation about the religious tradition from which he will arise. Will he be a pope of the Catholic Church? Will he be an imam leading people in the ways of Islam? Will he be a secularist enforcing the ideas of humanism and the belief that God is dead? Is there a unifying religious system that he might use to bring people of all faiths under his umbrella?

The answer is yes. It is the religion of climate change. What began as simple environmentalism and a push for good stewardship of the earth has become a new faith, complete with its own laws, creeds, and crusaders. Its apostles include liberal politicians, educators, the Hollywood left, and social media of every kind. Through their missionary work, the gospel of climate change has assimilated itself to the very roots of global culture. Because of how deeply it is entrenched, it crosses every border, whether national, political, generational, societal, or religious. The late theoretical physicist and mathematician Freeman Dyson described the entrenchment and universal acceptance of climate change in this way:

> Environmentalism has replaced secularism as the leading secular religion. And the ethics of environmentalism are fundamentally sound. Scientists and economists can agree with Buddhist monks and Christian activists that ruthless destruction of natural habitats is evil and careful preservation of birds and butterflies is good. The worldwide community of environmentalists—most of whom are not scientists—holds the moral high ground, and is guiding human societies toward a hopeful future. Environmentalism, as a religion of hope and respect for nature, is here to stay. This is a religion that we can all share, whether or not we believe that global warming is harmful.[27]

Following the aftermath of the rapture and the devastation of the Ezekiel 38 war, one man will come forward with a message of hope, not just for humanity but for the planet. His platform will boldly state that we have only one Earth, and everyone everywhere has a responsibility to protect it. In the hedonistic culture of the age, this is the one unifying cause that everyone can get behind and feel good about themselves as they make their little sacrifices to their great goddess, Gaia.

THE STAGE IS SET

If you have ever performed in a stage production, you know the feeling just prior to the show. The makeup is applied. The costumes are on. The sets are in place, and everyone is on their marks. All that needs to happen now is for the curtain to go up.

That is where we are when it comes to the rapture. As we've seen, all the sorrows or birth pangs that Jesus spoke of in the Olivet Discourse are active and growing in intensity. It is also clear that the world has shifted to a global mindset to such an extent that all that's missing for the antichrist's arrival is a red carpet.

Can I give you a date for the rapture or for when the tribulation will begin? I'm sorry, I can't. No one can. I can reassure you, though, that we are not only in the last generation, but we are in the time within the last generation in which everything is in place for the curtain to rise at any moment.

THE EMPEROR
AND THE POLITICIAN

A number of years ago, American comedian Jeff Foxworthy had a series of jokes that would conclude, "…you might be a redneck." Some examples:

> If you think the French Riviera is a foreign car, you might be a redneck.
>
> If you think a turtleneck is a key ingredient for soup, you might be a redneck.
>
> If you've ever made change in the offering plate, you might be a redneck.[28]

Now, I must admit that as an Israeli, I know next to nothing about people whose skin around their collar might lean toward the rosier side. The complexions where I come from typically range from olive to a rich medium brown. But I couldn't help but think about this comedy bit as I approach these next three chapters. We've spent a lot of time looking at why we are not currently in the tribulation. But for those of you reading this book who may not have taken that step of receiving Jesus as your Savior and Lord, I thought it might be helpful to let you know how you can be sure that the tribulation actually has begun.

SEVEN FULL YEARS OF WRATH

If you see the rise of the antichrist, you are definitely in the tribulation.

As we saw in chapter 6, there are many Christians who believe that the seven years of tribulation are divided between the relatively peaceful first three-and-a-half years and the second three-and-a-half years that are full of horrific judgments, known as the wrath of God. That is not a biblical doctrine. Think about it: What is preserving the world right now from going completely crazy? It is the Holy Spirit. He is the mediating factor as He indwells every believer, working through them to impact society. But when the rapture comes, the restraining work of the Holy Spirit will cease:

> Now you know what is restraining, that he may be revealed in his own time. For the mystery of lawlessness is already at work; only He who now restrains will do so until He is taken out of the way. And then the lawless one will be revealed, whom the Lord will consume with the breath of His mouth and destroy with the brightness of His coming (2 Thessalonians 2:6-8).

Currently, the world is not prepared for the rise of the antichrist. The influence of godly righteousness originating in the Holy Spirit and passing through the church is too great. But once the church goes and the Holy Spirit's restraining work with it, there will be nothing left to stem sin in global society. Can you imagine what the world will look like? Once the initial shock of millions of people disappearing wears off and the remaining population realizes who it is that is gone, there will be celebrations and dancing in the streets. The moral police have left the building! Every party needs a pooper, but now our poopers are all gone!

The cultural deterioration and degradation will be rapid and devastating. It will be a festival of ungodliness, chaos, death, deception, fear, and anger. There will no longer be any mediating factor that includes God's mercy, grace, love, hope, peace, and life. Instead, the one in charge is the same one who comes only "to steal, and to kill, and to destroy" (John 10:10). He is the one who will give the antichrist his power, his throne, and his authority.

This is why those who say that the first half of the tribulation will be nothing but calm seas are totally missing the tsunami that is rapidly approaching shore. Not only will that time be plagued with immorality, lawlessness, and violence, it will also experience the full venting of God's wrath. That the suffering extends through the entire final week, or seven years, of Daniel's prophecy is made clear by both the prophet himself and the apostle Paul.

The Hebrew word that Daniel uses for the time of God's punishment on the earth is זעם, *zaam*. In English, the word is translated "wrath, rage, indignation." That is what the world will experience in the final of Daniel's 70 weeks.

Daniel chapter 8 is where we find this word associated with the tribulation. The prophet had a vision in which he was along the Ulai canal, which was in Susa in modern-day Iran. He looked up and saw a ram charging around. It had two large horns, one bigger than the other, and it was fierce. He charged to the west, and everyone ran away. He charged to the north, and everyone ran away. He charged to the south, and, sure enough, everyone ran away. Nobody could stand up against this mighty ram.

Suddenly, the prophet heard a sound to his west. He turned and saw a male goat rushing toward the ram with such speed and power that his hooves never even touched the ground. Set right between the goat's eyes was a single horn, and it looked terrifying. By the time the ram saw the goat, it was too late. The collision must have been deafening. The ram's two mighty horns that had been so frightening were shattered, and the beast fell to the ground. Not content to let his vanquished foe slink away, the goat did a little touchdown dance, trampling his foe underhoof.

If you're thinking, *Weird dream, Daniel,* stay tuned. The goat was now all-powerful and he strutted around confident in his goaty strength. But in the midst of showing off his authority, his mighty horn broke. In its place grew four new horns, each one angling off in a different direction. Then out of that quartet of horns sprang up one more horn. It was just a little one, at least at first. But it began to grow, and it either spiraled or it had three tips because it pointed to the south, to the east, and to the west toward the Holy Land.

If you're thinking, *Even weirder dream, Daniel,* stay tuned. This horn kept growing and growing until it reached up into the heavens, where it brought down some of the heavenly host and trampled on them. It even went up against the "Prince of the host" (Daniel 8:11), and this horn stopped the daily sacrifices and desecrated the temple. It usurped the daily sacrifices on the altar so that the horn was now the recipient of the worship. Are you maybe getting an idea of who this horn is? The vision ends with the words, "And he cast truth down to the ground. He did all this and prospered" (v. 12).

Thankfully for Daniel and for us, the angel Gabriel was there to explain this wild vision. We'll get to his explanation, but first I want to look at how God's spokesangel introduced his description. First, he makes it clear that this vision is looking toward events that are far in the future: "He came near where I stood, and when he came I was afraid and fell on my face; but he said to me, 'Understand, son of man, that the vision refers to the time of the end'" (Daniel 8:17). Then he adds, "Look, I am making known to you what shall happen in the latter time of the indignation; for at the appointed time the end shall be" (v. 19). He's saying that this vision will have its greater fulfillment at the end of time. What part of the end of time? In the latter time of the indignation. Remember, indignation is another way of saying wrath, or *zaam*. The antichrist will declare himself to be god in the latter part of the wrath. If that temple desecration takes place halfway through the tribulation, then that means that the entire seven years must constitute the wrath of God. There is no easy first half of the tribulation.

It is this wrath from which Paul says we will be rescued. In the Greek New Testament, "wrath" is a translation of the word *orge*, and it is used 34 times. When we look at the Greek translation of Daniel's Hebrew, we see that *orge* is the word that was used to translate *zaam*. Therefore, when Paul used *orge* to describe God's wrath, he understood it to be the seven years described by the prophet Daniel.

So, when Paul wrote to a confused church in Thessalonica of "Jesus who delivers us from the wrath to come" (1 Thessalonians 1:10), he was speaking of the entire tribulation, not just the second half. And notice the preposition "from." Not "through" or "in" or "during." Jesus will deliver us *from* the wrath to come.

Why? Because the wrath is not for us. "For God did not appoint us to wrath, but to obtain salvation through our Lord Jesus Christ, who died for us, that whether we wake or sleep, we should live together with Him" (1 Thessalonians 5:9-10). He didn't say that God didn't appoint us to most of the wrath or half of the wrath. The full seven years of the wrath of God is not for the church.

DUAL FULFILLMENT

At the beginning of the tribulation—again, the full seven years—the antichrist will make his appearance. A typical misconception is that most of what we know about this servant of Satan is found in the New Testament. But, as we've just seen, there are clear prophecies of his arrival, his activities, and his eventual demise in Daniel's visions.

Like most other prophets such as Joel and Jeremiah, the messages given to Daniel have dual fulfillments. A great example of this is found within Isaiah's prophecies. King Ahaz of Judah was an evil man. He was an idol-worshipper who went so far as to place a pagan altar on the temple grounds next to the true altar. His depravity led him to even sacrifice his own son in the fires to a false god. Yet the Lord's love for His people was greater than the degeneracy of their actions and that of their monarch.

When the overwhelming forces of King Rezin of Aram and King Pekah of Israel came marching toward King Ahaz and his depleted army, God stepped in. He sent Isaiah and his son, Shear-jashub, to the king with a message. "Don't be afraid. I've got this. In fact, it won't be too much longer before the northern kingdom of Israel won't even exist anymore." The king's faith was weak, so the Lord offered to give him proof of His sincerity. But Ahaz, in his idolatrous rebellion, refused to ask for a sign, quite possibly because he had already decided to ignore God's promise and instead, seek help from the mighty Assyrian Empire.

The Lord determined to give the wayward king a sign of His faithfulness anyway. Isaiah brought His message, saying,

> Hear now, O house of David! Is it a small thing for you to weary men, but will you weary my God also? Therefore the Lord Himself will give you a sign: Behold, the virgin shall conceive and bear a Son, and shall call His name Immanuel. Curds and honey He shall eat, that He may know to refuse the evil and choose the good. For before the Child shall know to refuse the evil and choose the good, the land that you dread will be forsaken by both her kings. The LORD will bring the king of Assyria upon you and your people and your father's house—days that have not come since the day that Ephraim departed from Judah (Isaiah 7:13-17).

This was a good news, bad news prophecy. The good news was that by the time a certain young woman would marry, conceive, bear a son, and then wean the child, both King Rezin and King Pekah would be no more. "That is going to be My doing. That child will be the evidence of Immanuel—the fact that I am still with you, Judah." The bad news was that God knew they were still going to turn to Tiglath-pileser III of Assyria for help. "He'll come all right," God promised. "But he is going to plunder you and you are all going to become Assyria's vassals." Within just a few years, both sides of that prophecy came to pass.

But, as I'm sure you have already realized, there is also a distant fulfillment to Isaiah's prophecy. When he spoke for God, he was not just speaking of physical salvation for Judah, but of a spiritual Savior for all mankind. Joseph was betrothed to a young woman named Mary. But before they were wedded, she was found to be pregnant. Joseph was still trying to figure out how to end the betrothal without bringing more shame on his fiancée when he had an unexpected visitor.

> While he thought about these things, behold, an angel of the Lord appeared to him in a dream, saying, "Joseph, son of David, do not be afraid to take to you Mary your wife, for that which is conceived in her is of the Holy Spirit. And she will bring forth a Son, and you shall call His name JESUS, for He will save His people from their sins." So all this was done that it might be fulfilled which was spoken by the Lord through the prophet, saying: "Behold, the virgin shall be with child, and bear a Son, and they shall call His name Immanuel," which is translated, "God with us" (Matthew 1:20-23).

The prophecy given centuries earlier and realized by contemporary events had a later and much greater fulfillment when Jesus, the true "God with us," was born of a virgin. As we return to examine in greater detail Daniel 8, we must keep this dual fulfillment of prophecy in mind. There are those who say that his words were fulfilled in the actions of military leaders who rose within generations of Daniel's lifetime. They are exactly right. However, to then move the vision over to the "Prophecy Completely Fulfilled" side of the ledger would be premature. There is still much more to come. So, as we examine Daniel 8, we will look back into history. But we will also turn our eyes toward the future.

The Near Fulfillment

To truly understand future fulfillment, we need to make sense of the near fulfillment. Daniel's vision began with a ram:

> I lifted my eyes and saw, and there, standing beside the river, was a ram which had two horns, and the two horns were high; but one was higher than the other, and the higher one came up last. I saw the ram pushing westward, northward, and southward, so that no animal could withstand him; nor was there any that could deliver from his hand, but he did according to his will and became great (8:3-4).

This powerful animal represented the Medo-Persian, or Achaemenid, Empire. It was the Medo-Persians who finally had the strength, under Cyrus the Great, to overthrow the mighty Babylonian Empire less than three decades after the death of Babylon's great King Nebuchadnezzar. For more than two centuries after the Medo-Persians came to power, no one could stand against this powerful ram.

Then, in 333 BC, a goat came charging in. Young, powerful, and on a military roll, this character truly was the G.O.A.T.—Greatest of All Time—Alexander the Great, ruler of Macedon. The Macedonian

Empire rushed in with the single horn of Alexander leading the way and it headbutted the ram into oblivion:

> Suddenly a male goat came from the west, across the surface of the whole earth, without touching the ground; and the goat had a notable horn between his eyes. Then he came to the ram that had two horns, which I had seen standing beside the river, and ran at him with furious power. And I saw him confronting the ram; he was moved with rage against him, attacked the ram, and broke his two horns. There was no power in the ram to withstand him, but he cast him down to the ground and trampled him; and there was no one that could deliver the ram from his hand (vv. 5-7).

At the Battle of Issus in 333 BC, Alexander the Great defeated Darius III, fulfilling Daniel's two-century-old prophecy. Eventually, the conquering hero made it to Jerusalem and walked to the Temple Mount. The high priest was there waiting for him and said something to the effect of "Welcome, Mr. the Great. We've been expecting you."

Surprised, Alexander responded, "What you talkin' 'bout, Willis?" We don't have the transcript, so his exact words may have been slightly different.

In reply, the high priest opened the Scriptures and showed him Daniel's prophecy that Greece, or Macedon, would take over the Medo-Persians. Alexander was so amazed that the Holy Scriptures had prophesied about him that he ordered the temple of the Jews not to be destroyed. It became the only temple to a foreign religion whose destruction he did not order. Who knows what this great conqueror might have accomplished if he had been given more time? Instead, seven years after he conquered the Persians, he died under mysterious circumstances at the age of 32 in the Babylonian palace of former king Nebuchadnezzar.

With the single horn gone, the goat sprouted four more:

> Therefore the male goat grew very great; but when he
> became strong, the large horn was broken, and in place
> of it four notable ones came up toward the four winds of
> heaven. And out of one of them came a little horn which
> grew exceedingly great toward the south, toward the east,
> and toward the Glorious Land (vv. 8-9).

With youth often comes a feeling of invincibility. Alexander likely thought he had decades ahead of him before he would have to consider who would take over after him. So, when he unexpectedly died, there was no plan of succession established. Before his death, he had divided oversight of his empire amongst four of his generals, Cassander, Lysimachus, Ptolemy, and Seleucus, making them satraps or governors. After the usual betrayals, assassinations, and the like, they each essentially took over their regions. The big horn was gone and replaced by four horns, exactly as Daniel's prophecy had said.

For our story, we only care about one of these four, Seleucus. He had been given oversight of Syria, Mesopotamia, and other areas to the east. It is out of this horn that, according to Daniel's angel, a little horn would grow. Seleucus established his rule for the next 40 years and became the founder of the Seleucid Empire. Ninety years passed with the Seleucid Empire having its ups and downs. Then, Antiochus III the Great took the reins. Prior to his ascension, the empire had been going through one of its down times with military defeats by Ptolemy III of Egypt, regions breaking off and declaring independence, and even familial civil war and strife. When Antiochus III took over as emperor, he changed all that. He was a warrior whose victories put some of the shine back on the Seleucid crest.

At that time, Jerusalem was situated within the squishy border region between the Seleucid and the Ptolemaic Empires, so it would occasionally pass from one team to the other. After Antiochus III rose to the throne, the Jews decided they were tired of Ptolemaic oversight and opened the gates of Jerusalem to the Seleucid ruler. He promptly chased the Egyptians out. Appreciative of what the Jews did, Antiochus III was friendly to them and rewarded their loyalty. Antiochus III was not the little horn. He only set the stage for the little horn, his son Antiochus IV.

A dozen years after the death of his father, Antiochus IV was declared emperor. The year was 175 BC, and he would rule until his death 9 years later at age 51. Antiochus IV was never in line for the throne. After his father's death, his brother Seleucus IV Philopator became emperor. But 12 years into his rule, he was assassinated. His son, Demetrius I Soter, was next in line. However, he was only 10 years old and was being held as a hostage in Rome. Seizing his opportunity, Antiochus IV declared himself emperor and pulled in enough support to usurp the throne from his absent young nephew. This kind of deception was the hallmark of his reign, and fits perfectly with his description in Daniel: "Through his cunning he shall cause deceit to prosper under his rule; and he shall exalt himself in his heart" (v. 25).

Today, when people are described as having a god complex, it typically means that they are narcissistic and feel a strong sense of entitlement, superiority, and infallibility. Antiochus IV had a true god complex, meaning that he actually thought he was God. He designated himself Epiphanes, which means "God manifest." And because he was now officially "God," the emperor decided it was a good idea for everyone to start worshipping him.

While not a clinical term, I think it is safe to say that Antiochus IV was nuts. Instead of Epiphanes, many of those around him called him Epimenes, or "mad man," although likely not to his face. All the regions under the umbrella of the Seleucids were polytheistic, meaning they followed many gods. So, when Antiochus demanded their worship, they said, "Sure, why not? Put him on the list."

There was one ethnic group, however, who believed that there was only one God. The Jews had been vassals to the Seleucids ever since they had opened the gates of Jerusalem to Antiochus's father. For them, to worship a man would be the worst of all sins, going against the first and greatest commandment, "You shall have no other gods before Me" (Exodus 20:3). A violent man already, this refusal opened the floodgates of the emperor's madness. His soldiers poured into Jerusalem and thousands of Jews were slaughtered in the streets. Thousands more were taken captive and sold into slavery.

In his interpretation of Daniel's vision, the angel Gabriel said this of the little horn:

> His power shall be mighty, but not by his own power;
> he shall destroy fearfully,
> and shall prosper and thrive;
> he shall destroy the mighty, and also the holy people (v. 24).

The destruction wrought by Antiochus IV caused him to be known in rabbinical sources by the name *HaRasha*, "the wicked." This wannabe god determined that if the Jews weren't going to worship him, then they weren't going to worship at all. He forbade the people from following the mandates of the Judaic law. He outlawed the Jewish sacrifices in the temple and instead, burned pagan offerings on the altar. Then, in the straw that broke the camel's back, he desecrated the temple by dedicating it to Zeus.

A rebellion arose under the leadership of Judas Maccabeus. This military genius defeated Seleucid's army until the empire was finally driven out. The temple was restored and rededicated to the true God, giving birth to Hanukkah, which means "rededication." Three years after the advent of the rebellion, Antiochus IV died of an illness in Tabae, modern-day Isfahan, Iran.

It is unimaginable the horrors that Daniel must have witnessed in his vision. It is no wonder he concluded by writing, "And I, Daniel, fainted and was sick for days; afterward I arose and went about the king's business. I was astonished by the vision, but no one understood it" (v. 27). The most frightening fact to remember about the remarkably precise realization of Daniel's vision is that it was only the near fulfillment. The future, greater fulfillment is still yet to come.

The Future Fulfillment

Antiochus IV was a bad man. The man who is still to come will be far worse. When David came home after routing the Philistines, the women danced and sang, "Saul has slain his thousands, and David his ten thousands" (1 Samuel 18:7). In the future, a new song could be sung: "Antiochus has slain his ten thousands, and the antichrist his ten millions." The similarities between the two men are rife; the antichrist just exponentially ups the level of evil.

Antiochus IV fiercely persecuted the Jews, foreshadowing the horrific persecution with which the antichrist will target Israel in the future. The emperor's level of sinister intrigue in his rise to power portrays how the antichrist will use dishonesty and violence in his future climb to the top. Just as Antiochus was empowered by Satan, so will the antichrist be. And just as he prospered for a time, so will the antichrist. The antichrist will advance through deceit, just as Antiochus did.

The Seleucid emperor was infamous for his attempt to portray himself as divinity, calling himself Epiphanes. The future antichrist will also claim to be God, as we'll see in a moment. Antiochus spoke "pompous words against the Most High" (Daniel 7:25), while the antichrist will be "given a mouth speaking great things and blasphemies, and he was given authority to continue for forty-two months" (Revelation 13:5). And on both accounts, the motive for relentlessly persecuting the Jews is a passionate disdain for the one true God.

Antiochus was not killed by a man, but by a disease. The antichrist will also not be killed by a man, but by Jesus Himself.

The great theologian and Oxford University professor of mathematics, John Lennox, wrote:

> In Antiochus there were the seeds of an evil that will gestate and come to its fearful fruition in a time yet to come. Antiochus and the events of his time, therefore, form a prototype or thought model of the future, which will help Daniel and us imagine what is to come—and to be aware of similar tendencies in our own day.[29]

The Seleucid emperor gives us just a taste of what is to come. When the true antichrist arrives, he will come with the full power of Satan at his disposal.

In Matthew 24, Jesus directed His disciples to the prophet Daniel, saying, "'When you see the "abomination of desolation," spoken of by Daniel the prophet, standing in the holy place' (whoever reads, let him understand), 'then let those who are in Judea flee to the mountains'" (vv. 15-16). In other words, "When you see the future antichrist, the one Daniel talked about, the one that is much greater than Antiochus IV, the one who will have a huge sculpture of himself standing in the temple and will demand that the world worship him as if he is god, you are definitely in the tribulation!"

Paul used words similar to those in Daniel when he wrote:

> Let no one deceive you by any means; for that Day will not come unless the falling away comes first, and the man of sin is revealed, the son of perdition, who opposes and exalts himself above all that is called God or that is worshiped, so that he sits as God in the temple of God, showing himself that he is God (2 Thessalonians 2:3-4).

When the man of sin is revealed and he is sitting in the temple claiming to be God, you are definitely in the tribulation. Now, there are some of you out there who are likely saying, "But, Amir, that won't happen until halfway through the tribulation. How can I know now if the antichrist is rising to power now?" Great question. A very simple answer for the believer is you can't. Or, at least, you won't.

Olympus Mons is the largest volcano in our solar system. From rim to rim, it is the size of the state of Arizona.[30] However, if this massive volcano were to erupt, I would never know it. Why? Because it is on Mars, and I don't live on Mars. When the antichrist comes to power, it will be here on earth. I, however, will never know it because I will have changed residences by that time and will be living in a place prepared by my Lord in heaven specially for me.

For those of you, though, who may have come across this book in the house of your Christian neighbor who recently disappeared along with millions of others, and now you're raiding their pantry trying to scrounge up some food because the supply lines to the grocery stores have collapsed, let me first say help yourself. Your neighbor isn't going to need any of that stuff. And don't forget the perishables in the refrigerator.

If you, my friend of the future, are wondering if that guy who has suddenly shown up on the world stage is the antichrist, then chances are the answer is yes. Just to be sure, let me ask you two questions: Has there been a war in Israel where Russia and its allies got miraculously trounced? And are all the Israelis, who don't normally follow anyone who isn't Jewish, suddenly giving their allegiance to that guy you're wondering about? If the answers to those questions are yes, then he is certainly the antichrist, and you are most definitely in the tribulation.

But there is still hope for you. The Jews won't recognize the antichrist for who he is until halfway through the seven years, and the rest of the population will remain clueless throughout. You, however, can change your eternity now. You can see the antichrist for who he is, and you can see the real Christ for who He is. Give your heart to Jesus Christ while there is still time. Believe me, He is ready to give you eternal life. Sadly, the years ahead of you will be extremely difficult, and it is very likely you will not live to see the end. Your comfort, however, comes from knowing that when this time of global tribulation ends for you, eternal life awaits in the presence of your Lord and Savior.

1:0

A PLACE TO
CALL HOME

God wants to dwell with His creation. How fantastic is it to hear that? All those times when you feel like you've let Him down or that He must be so disappointed in you that He's ready to cut you off completely? You couldn't be further from the truth. The reason He created each one of us is so we could have a loving relationship with Him.

It is this desire that led to Him causing places to be built that would represent His presence among humanity. It is one of these buildings, a temple, that is the second of the signs that you have missed the rapture and are now in the tribulation. But what temple is this, and why does God have temples at all? Are they really necessary in this day and age? For the church, who, as we have already seen, is "a chosen generation, a royal priesthood, a holy nation, His own special people" (1 Peter 2:9), the temple is not a necessity. We have the Holy Spirit indwelling us, so there is no need for an external representation of God's presence. Yet once the church is removed from earth, the temple will be rebuilt. In fact, two temples will be built post-rapture. As the church, we will not be around to see the one, but we will worship God and celebrate our Savior at the other.

Right now, there is not a temple in Jerusalem, but one is coming. If you see a temple in Jerusalem, you are definitely in the tribulation.

GOD WANTS TO DWELL WITH HIS CREATION

In the beginning, the Creator fellowshipped with His creation. In the Garden of Eden, we get a glimpse of the close relationship that once was, and the devastation of that bond being broken:

> They heard the sound of the LORD God walking in the garden in the cool of the day, and Adam and his wife hid themselves from the presence of the LORD God among the trees of the garden. Then the LORD God called to Adam and said to him, "Where are you?" So he said, "I heard Your voice in the garden, and I was afraid because I was naked; and I hid myself" (Genesis 3:8-10).

How wonderful it was that God wanted to commune so closely with Adam and Eve. How tragic it was that the selfishness of sin destroyed that closeness. Once sinful rebellion entered the world, all man was interested in was fulfilling his own desires and hiding from God.

But then the people of that time took it a step further. Not only did they want to hide from God, they wanted to replace Him. They gathered on the plain of Shinar and decided to build a tower that would reach up into the heavens. God recognized their arrogant motives and stepped in:

> The LORD came down to see the city and the tower which the sons of men had built. And the LORD said, "Indeed the people are one and they all have one language, and this is what they begin to do; now nothing that they propose to do will be withheld from them. Come, let Us go

down and there confuse their language, that they may not understand one another's speech." So the LORD scattered them abroad from there over the face of all the earth, and they ceased building the city. Therefore its name is called Babel, because there the LORD confused the language of all the earth; and from there the LORD scattered them abroad over the face of all the earth (Genesis 11:5-9).

Think about it: God created the world. Two chapters later, we told Him we'd rather do things our way. Then eight chapters after that, we decided we wanted to run the whole show. But God never gave up on us. Still, He wanted a relationship with His small-minded, wayward children. So, He chose Abraham, and decided that He would show the world just how special a close relationship with Him could be. "I will set My tabernacle among you, and My soul shall not abhor you. I will walk among you and be your God, and you shall be My people" (Leviticus 26:11-12). All it would take to maintain this closeness was for Abraham's descendants to follow God, obeying Him and worshipping Him only. Sounds like a great deal! What could possibly go wrong?

The Tabernacle—the Pre-Temple

As a symbol of the special and intimate relationship God had with Israel, the Lord told Moses to build a tabernacle. In Hebrew, we don't actually use that word. We call it the *ohel moed*—the "tent of meeting"—because that is what took place there. It was where deity met humanity and communed with them. When the Lord gave the instructions for the building of the tabernacle, He told Moses, "Let them make Me a sanctuary, that I may dwell among them" (Exodus 25:8). Once again, that's God's heart.

Moses, in return, desired that same closeness with God, so he "took his tent and pitched it outside the camp, far from the camp, and called it the tabernacle of meeting" (Exodus 33:7). Whenever he wanted to spend time with God, he would enter the tabernacle, and "the pillar of cloud descended and stood at the door of the tabernacle, and the LORD talked with Moses…So the LORD spoke to Moses face to face, as a man speaks to his friend" (vv. 9, 11). God's presence was in the cloud, and He conversed with His chosen leader.

What did God and Moses talk about when they were "face to face"? If we read just a little further in Exodus 33, we get a glimpse into a conversation inside the tent of meeting. God had told Moses that He was going to send the prophet and the people on ahead. However, the Lord would be staying behind, because these stiff-necked people were pushing all the wrong buttons with Him.

Moses, however, was having none of it, telling God that he desperately needed Him to come with them. God, in His ever-deep compassion, responded, "My Presence will go with you, and I will give you rest" (v. 14). But Moses wanted to plead his case a little more so that God would truly understand how necessary it was for Him to be with them:

> If Your Presence does not go with us, do not bring us up
> from here. For how then will it be known that Your people
> and I have found grace in Your sight, except You go with
> us? So we shall be separate, Your people and I, from all
> the people who are upon the face of the earth (vv. 15-16).

If that's not sweet aroma to the Lord, I don't know what is. This is exactly what He had wanted from the beginning of creation—His people to love Him and desire a close relationship. "So the LORD said to Moses, 'I will also do this thing that you have spoken; for you have found grace in My sight, and I know you by name'" (v. 17).

Eventually, though, Moses passed from the scene. Then Moses' faithful successor, Joshua, also died. Now in the Promised Land, the people forgot about what God had done for them, freeing them from Pharaoh's hand, parting the Red Sea, and providing for them in the wilderness. The time of the Judges descended upon the land, a morally compromised time when "everyone did what was right in his own eyes" (Judges 17:6).

The First Temple—Solomon's Temple

At some point, the Israelites realized that this whole system of semi-controlled anarchy was getting them nowhere. But rather than turning back to God for direction, they pleaded for a king to lead them. God told them, "Guys, this is not a good idea." But they replied, "Says You. We think it's a great idea. So, give us a king." And that's what God did, providing for them the sin-filled, weak-willed King Saul. In other words, he was a king who mirrored the people.

Saul's reign went about as well as expected. Then God, in His compassion, decided to give them a different kind of king. Rather than one who was cut from their same cloth, this king was a man after God's own heart. King David sat on the throne and set the standard for all kings to come.

One day, out of his love and devotion for the Lord, David determined that he was going to build Him a temple so that He wouldn't have to dwell in that old tabernacle tent any more. God said, "I appreciate the offer, but you're not the guy. I'm going to have your son, Solomon, build it." And that's exactly what King Solomon did. The temple was spectacular! It shined like gold, was smooth like marble, and smelled like cedar. It was truly a holy house fit for the Creator God! A place so amazing it would move people to say, "Wow! God is there! Let's go worship Him!"

And that's what they did…for a time.

Sadly, though, it wasn't long before deception began permeating the house of God. I'm not just talking about the land or the nation in general. Evil slithered onto the Temple Mount and into the temple itself. The worship of other gods invaded the holy site.

Before the fall of Jerusalem, Ezekiel was taken by an angel to see why God was going to judge the city. The angel brought the prophet to the temple, where he saw 70 elders of the house of Israel offering incense up to gods and idols that had been drawn on the walls. But that wasn't the worst of it:

> He said to me, "Turn again, and you will see greater abominations that they are doing." So He brought me to the door of the north gate of the LORD's house; and to my dismay, women were sitting there weeping for Tammuz (Ezekiel 8:13-14).

In Babylonian mythology, Tammuz was a young god who was married to the goddess Ishtar. She betrayed him and he was murdered, causing great sorrow amongst the women of the world. Because he was killed in the autumn, the falling of the leaves and the dying of the vegetation during that season were reminders of Tammuz's tragic fate, causing women throughout the pagan world to weep for him. This is what was taking place in the temple of the one true God.

But that wasn't the worst of it either:

> Then He said to me, "Have you seen this, O son of man? Turn again, you will see greater abominations than these." So He brought me into the inner court of the LORD's house; and there, at the door of the temple of the LORD, between the porch and the altar, were about twenty-five men with their backs toward the temple of the LORD and their faces toward the east, and they were worshiping the sun toward the east (vv. 15-16).

Can you picture that in your mind? The house of the Lord is right there, but their backs are turned toward the presence of God.

Instead, they are facing the sun, worshipping it as it rises in the east. That depicts the outright rebellion of the human heart that was a problem not only then, but still prevails today. It is no wonder that only two chapters later, the glory of the Lord rose up and departed from the temple.

Finally, God had enough. He "sent warnings to them by His messengers, rising up early and sending them, because He had compassion on His people and on His dwelling place. But they mocked the messengers of God, despised His words, and scoffed at His prophets, until the wrath of the LORD arose against His people, till there was no remedy" (2 Chronicles 36:15-16). In 586 BC, the Babylonians marched in and tore the temple to the ground.

The Second Temple—Herod's Temple

One person watching the Babylonian invasion was the old prophet Jeremiah. He had spent his entire life warning kings and his fellow citizens that this day was coming. For Jeremiah, any hope of peace in Jerusalem during his lifetime was gone. However, he did know that peace, and even restoration, would come. Through this prophet, the Lord had promised, "This whole land shall be a desolation and an astonishment, and these nations shall serve the king of Babylon seventy years" (Jeremiah 25:11). The Babylonian exile was not to be a permanent state. It had a beginning, and it would have an end.

Why 70 years? When Moses was with God on Mount Sinai, the Lord had instituted an agricultural Sabbath for their future Promised Land:

> When you come into the land which I give you, then the land shall keep a sabbath to the LORD. Six years you shall sow your field, and six years you shall prune your vineyard, and gather its fruit; but in the seventh year there shall be a sabbath of solemn rest for the land, a sabbath

to the Lord. You shall neither sow your field nor prune your vineyard (Leviticus 25:2-4).

At some point after the Hebrews came into the land, this commandment, which was instituted for the health of the soil, was forgotten. In fact, for 490 years it was set aside. Now that Sabbath bill was coming due. Every seventh year for 490 years equals 70 years. God knew what the soil needed, and He was going to have His fallow Sabbath years one way or another.

The clock ticked away during the exile, until one day the alarm rang and King Cyrus of Persia, the empire that had made Babylon pay for its mistreatment of the Jews, issued a decree allowing the people of Judah to go back home. A contingent of returnees under the leadership of Zerubbabel, the grandson of Judah's King Jehoiachin, migrated back to Jerusalem and the surrounding area. They began the process of rebuilding the temple, but faced much opposition and many setbacks. Through great perseverance, two decades later, the returned exiles finally completed the second—yet much less opulent—temple.

Hundreds of years passed before the Hasmonean Dynasty, who defeated the Greeks in the first century, expanded the second temple. Several more decades went by, then Herod the Great took the throne. He was a builder, and there was nothing he loved more than a massive construction project. Much of Herod the Great's attention was given to the temple, and he greatly expanded the temple platform by building long retaining walls that made the area much bigger.

With the temple restored and enlarged, God made His return. However, His reappearance was very different from His departure. He did not return in a cloud or a pillar of fire. Rather, His homecoming was much more subtle:

Now when the days of her purification according to the law of Moses were completed, they brought [Jesus] to

Jerusalem to present Him to the Lord (as it is written in the law of the Lord, "Every male who opens the womb shall be called holy to the LORD"), and to offer a sacrifice according to what is said in the law of the Lord, "A pair of turtledoves or two young pigeons" (Luke 2:22-24).

With the first temple, the people didn't realize that God had left the building. With the second temple, they didn't realize that He was back. There was also something else they didn't understand about this second temple: The rules were changing. The temple didn't mean what it used to mean.

As Jesus was passing through Samaria with His disciples, He stopped to rest by a well. A woman came to draw some water, and Jesus engaged her in conversation. The woman soon realized that she was speaking to no ordinary man. She said to Him, "Sir, I perceive that You are a prophet. Our fathers worshiped on this mountain, and you Jews say that in Jerusalem is the place where one ought to worship" (John 4:19-20). It is in Jesus' response to this woman that we see the new view of the temple:

Jesus said to her, "Woman, believe Me, the hour is coming when you will neither on this mountain, nor in Jerusalem, worship the Father. You worship what you do not know; we know what we worship, for salvation is of the Jews. But the hour is coming, and now is, when the true worshipers will worship the Father in spirit and truth; for the Father is seeking such to worship Him. God is Spirit, and those who worship Him must worship in spirit and truth" (vv. 21-24).

God is not physical, and He does not dwell in a physical building made by human hands. His dwelling is in that which is God-made. What is His God-made dwelling? It is you and me. "Do you not know that you are the temple of God and that the Spirit of God dwells in you?" (1 Corinthians 3:16). So, while it is nice to have a temple to remind us about God, and while it would be pretty to look at, we don't need to go to a building to worship Him—that includes your church. Wherever we are is where the temple of God is, which means we can worship Him at any moment of any day.

Because this second temple was just a building, it too didn't last. As Jesus and His disciples were departing the temple area one day, they pointed out to Him how amazing were the various structures on the mount. Jesus surprised them by saying, "Do you not see all these things? Assuredly, I say to you, not one stone shall be left here upon another, that shall not be thrown down" (Matthew 24:2).

As a tour guide who spent more than 20 years leading people around Jerusalem, I used to take them to the Herodian street. From there you are able to see the stones that were thrown from the Temple Mount less than four decades after the Lord made that statement. The smallest stones weigh two-and-a-half tons, and the largest reach more than 600 tons. They're huge! They serve as visual, tangible proof that the prophecies that come from the mouth of God always come to pass.

The ultimate destruction of this second temple wasn't just a New Testament concept. Daniel was taken as a young man from Judah to Babylon. There, he was trained, made a eunuch, and incorporated into the court of King Nebuchadnezzar. Because of his wisdom and dependence upon God, he was rapidly elevated to a position of power and influence. As a prophet, Daniel received visions from God and, occasionally, angelic visitations. One day, as he was praying, the angel Gabriel came to him with a message from the Lord:

> Seventy weeks are determined
> for your people and for your holy city,
> to finish the transgression,
> to make an end of sins,

to make reconciliation for iniquity,
to bring in everlasting righteousness,
to seal up vision and prophecy,
and to anoint the Most Holy.

Know therefore and understand,
that from the going forth of the command
to restore and build Jerusalem
until Messiah the Prince,
there shall be seven weeks and sixty-two weeks;
the street shall be built again, and the wall,
even in troublesome times (Daniel 9:24-25).

Daniel received a vision of the future of Israel and Jerusalem. Gabriel told him that the moment King Artaxerxes would release Nehemiah to go and rebuild Jerusalem, it was time to start counting—7 weeks and 62 weeks, which by my math equals 69 weeks. Every week is a period of 7 years. Every year includes 360 days—remember, Daniel was a Jew, so he went by lunar years. Sixty-nine times 7 times 360 equals 173,880 days. I'll do the calendar work for you and tell you that if you add that number of days to the date of Artaxerxes's decree, it will place you on April 6, AD 32, the day Jesus rode a donkey into Jerusalem to the cries of "Blessed is He who comes in the name of the Lord!" (Matthew 21:9). What a wonderful celebration, and it would have been perfect if Gabriel had stopped there. But he continued:

After the sixty-two weeks
Messiah shall be cut off, but not for Himself;
and the people of the prince who is to come
shall destroy the city and the sanctuary (v. 26).

Jesus, the Messiah, was cut off—killed—but not because of anything that He had done. He died as part of the Father's plan for the remission of our sins. Then, in AD 70, the "prince," Titus, son of the Roman emperor Vespasian, laid siege to Jerusalem, eventually invading the city, razing it, and utterly destroying the temple. But is Titus really the prince that is being talked about here? He may be the shadow of this prophecy's fulfillment, but the substance goes far beyond just a son of a Roman emperor. As we look at the greater context, we see that there is one who is still yet to come whose vision, like that of Titus and his father Vespasian, is for the destruction of the Jews.

Two temples have been built, and two temples have been destroyed. But there are still two more to go.

The Third Temple—the Tribulation Temple

If ever you are at a point in Scripture where you are unsure of what is being said, one good piece of advice is to keep on reading. It is as we progress through the rest of Gabriel's message to Daniel that we find the identity of the prince mentioned in verse 26:

> Then he shall confirm a covenant with many for one week;
> but in the middle of the week
> he shall bring an end to sacrifice and offering.
> And on the wing of abominations shall be one who
>   makes desolate,
> even until the consummation, which is determined,
> is poured out on the desolate (v. 27).

He begins with the word "then," meaning that this will take place after the destruction of the city and the sanctuary (as mentioned in the previous verse). There are many who say that verses 26 and 27 are both referring to the destruction of Jerusalem in AD 70. They then rope in Revelation and say that it too describes Titus's razing of the city and demolishing of the temple. But that is not allowed either by the adverb "then" or a literal interpretation of Scripture. Verse 27 and the events of Revelation 4 onward must take place in the future during Daniel's 70th week. It is in that final set of seven years that "he," meaning "the prince," will bring an end to sacrifice and offering.

Who is the "he"? As we saw in the last chapter, it is the antichrist. And if he is able to end sacrifices and offerings halfway through the seven years of the tribulation, what must exist in Jerusalem during that time? A third temple! Paul wrote to the Thessalonians of this next temple and its desecration by the coming antichrist:

> Now, brethren, concerning the coming of our Lord Jesus Christ and our gathering together to Him, we ask you, not to be soon shaken in mind or troubled, either by spirit or by word or by letter, as if from us, as though the day of Christ had come. Let no one deceive you by any means; for that Day will not come unless the falling away comes first, and the man of sin is revealed, the son of perdition, who opposes and exalts himself above all that is called God or that is worshiped, so that he sits as God in the temple of God, showing himself that he is God (2 Thessalonians 2:1-4).

If you've heard something in your spirit or by word or by letter or by email or by YouTube or by social media post that tells you that the day of Christ has come and the tribulation is already here, relax! You've heard wrong. Do you see a temple in Jerusalem? If you do, then you need to get your vision checked. There is no third temple yet. In addition, Paul said that if you haven't witnessed the falling away and you haven't seen the antichrist, then don't worry, because the seven years have yet to begin.

Given the current climate between the Jews and the Arabs, can you imagine a third temple being built today on the Temple Mount? The first day of construction would see rioting of unprecedented proportions, while thousands of rockets would immediately fly into Israel from Gaza, Lebanon, and Syria. The only possible way for a temple rebuild to happen would be if someone were able to bring peace between the two parties. The man of peace who will be able to accomplish this feat is the antichrist. And the deal that he presents will be unlike anything that has been offered in the past. In Gabriel's announcement to Daniel that the prince will "confirm a covenant with many for one week" (Daniel 9:27), the Hebrew word for "confirm" is *higbir*. This word speaks of an agreement that is stronger than just a confirmation. It means "to increase, to step up, to do something greater from the usual to the unusual."

So far, there has been no peace deal offered to the Jews that will allow them to rebuild the temple. In order to increase the deal, to make it spectacular, to elevate it to the *higbir* level, what will the antichrist offer? You guessed it—a small parcel of prime real estate upon which a temple can be built. If he can work out that deal, every Jew in Israel will rise and call him blessed!

I'm no architect. I'm also not a prophet, so don't take this as coming from the Lord. There is a vacant area on the Temple Mount just north of the Dome of the Rock. In that stretch of ground is a little dome where some Jews believe the Holy of Holies used to be. Also, that space is in perfect alignment with where the Golden Gate—or the Eastern Gate—is today. So, I'm saying maybe, just maybe, that will be the site of the third temple.

Ultimately, I don't care where the third temple will be. I won't be here to see it. What's interesting is that I find so many Christians going absolutely crazy over every little piece of news that is even remotely related to the building of the next temple. Recently, a report circulated that a Texan had discovered five red heifers that he said fit the bill for the consecration of a new temple. He ended up flying them all the way to Israel, with a Christian organization footing the bill. My email inbox blew up! "Is the temple about to be built? Does this mean the rapture is about to happen? Are we now in the tribulation?" My responses have been, "I don't know. I don't know. And no!" Why is everyone going so crazy about red cows? Don't get me wrong, I've got nothing against cows no matter what color they are. Dry-aged then given a nice sear, they're one of my favorite animals.

Everyone in the church needs to relax about the third temple. It has nothing to do with us. It will survive until the end of the tribulation, but not beyond. Zechariah prophesied what will happen when Jesus returns at the end of the seven years of wrath:

> In that day His feet will stand on the Mount of Olives,
> which faces Jerusalem on the east.
> and the Mount of Olives shall be split in two,
> from east to west,
> making a very large valley;
> half of the mountain shall move toward the north
> and half of it toward the south (Zechariah 14:4).

When the Mount of Olives is split in two, a valley will open from the east to the west. What is west of the Mount of Olives, just on the other side of the narrow Kidron Valley? The Temple Mount. The entire area that is so precious to both the Jews and the Arabs will be completely destroyed.

The Fourth Temple—the Millennial Temple

I will touch only briefly on these last two sections because they are going beyond the time frame of our book. However, to fully wrap up this temple subject, we need to tie on a ribbon and add a pretty bow.

When Jesus returns, He will establish His kingdom in Jerusalem: "The LORD of hosts will reign on Mount Zion and in Jerusalem and before His elders, gloriously" (Isaiah 24:23). Once again, the holy city will be the head of all cities and Israel will be the head of all nations.

And in Jerusalem will be built a fourth temple, one much greater than any that has ever been seen on earth before.

Twenty-five years into the captivity of Israel, Ezekiel had a vision in which he was taken to a high mountain. There, he met a bronze-looking man with a measuring rod in his hand. This man said to Ezekiel, "Son of man, look with your eyes and hear with your ears, and fix your mind on everything I show you; for you were brought here so that I might show them to you. Declare to the house of Israel everything you see" (Ezekiel 40:4). Then the man proceeded to measure out, in a systematic and detailed manner, an enormous temple. This is the structure to which we will gather to worship during the 1,000-year reign of the King of kings and the Lord of lords. But even that temple won't last.

At the end of the millennium, Satan will be released from the abyss. He will gather his armies so he can attempt a last-chance victory against the Creator. But this plan will fail, just like all the others. The devil and his demons will be cast into the lake of fire for eternity. Then will come the second resurrection, which will lead to the Great White Throne judgment that we learned about earlier. Once all the judging is done and everyone is where they belong based on whether they received the free gift of salvation through Jesus Christ's shed blood on the cross, the end will come for this planet and the heavens surrounding it.

God Is the Temple—Eternity

Then there will be new heavens, a new earth, and a new Jerusalem. Inside this new holy city, there will be no temple, for a very good reason. In John's vision of eternity, he wrote, "I saw no temple in it, for the Lord God Almighty and the Lamb are its temple" (Revelation 21:22). How beautiful is that? In the Garden of Eden, there was no need for a temple because God walked among His creation. In the new heavens and new earth, there will be no need for a temple because the Lord and the Lamb will walk among their creation.

HAVE YOU MADE YOUR DECISION?

Remember, God wants fellowship with His children. The Savior's desire is to abide with us, and He wants us to abide with Him. Make your decision now to take Him up on His offer of salvation as a free gift. Then you, too, can look forward to when you will walk with the Lord in the cool of the day in His new heavens and new earth.

WRATH ON DISPLAY

Thus far, we have seen that if you turn on your television and the antichrist is on the screen, standing in front of the newly built temple in Jerusalem, you are definitely in the tribulation. But the antichrist and the temple are just two of the many indicators that the rapture has passed you over and you are now in the seven years of God's wrath. Once again, I must emphasize that if you are part of the church, you will not experience any of what you are about to read.

By part of the church, I don't mean that you attend a church. Standing in a church building doesn't make you a Christian any more than standing in a Jewish deli makes you kosher. The church is not a building, a denomination, or a religion. The church is made up of people, wherever they may be at any given moment, who have accepted Jesus Christ as their Savior and Lord, thereby receiving the free gift of salvation that comes through Jesus' death and resurrection. If that describes you, what follows should not bring you fear, only sorrow for your unsaved loved ones and motivation to tell them how they can escape this fate. If you have not committed yourself to Christ, however, then you should be terrified, because what I am about to describe to you is constrained by the limits of the English language. The reality will be much, much worse.

If you see the following events taking place around you, you are most definitely in the tribulation.

SUPERNATURAL ACTIVITIES

One reason that the world will follow after the antichrist is that he will be empowered by Satan to carry out the supernatural. Paul warned, "The coming of the lawless one is according to the working of Satan, with all power, signs, and lying wonders, and with all unrighteous deception among those who perish, because they did not receive the love of the truth, that they might be saved" (2 Thessalonians 2:9-10).

Imagine you are at a political rally. As the candidate wraps up his speech, he swirls his hand in the air. Clouds form above him and spin. Then lightning flashes and thunder rolls. "Vote for me," he says, "because I have the power to do what I say I'm going to do!" Upon seeing this, those of us who have a spiritual foundation that enables us to recognize dark spiritual activities would run the other way. But those without that kind of foundation would be in awe. They would probably think, *The world is such a mess right now, no ordinary man can put it all back together. But this is no ordinary man!*

Not only will the antichrist have supernatural powers, but so will his sidekick—the false prophet. These days, he would be known as the antichrist's hype man. His job is to get people's eyes on the main act so that they'll worship him:

> He performs great signs, so that he even makes fire come down from heaven on the earth in the sight of men. And he deceives those who dwell on the earth by those signs which he was granted to do in the sight of the beast, telling those who dwell on the earth to make an image to the beast who was wounded by the sword and lived (Revelation 13:13-14).

If you've got an unruly crowd around you and you want to get their attention, calling down fire from heaven is a pretty good way to do it. I'm sure a lot of high school teachers are wishing they could do the same trick. Political leaders who are performing impossible wonders—that's a good sign that you are in the tribulation.

But it's not just the bad guys who will be doing miracles. If each night the news gives an update on two obnoxious, poorly dressed men who have planted themselves in front of the newly built temple and won't stop talking about repentance, then you may want to keep your eye on them. Chances are someone is going to make an attempt on their lives. It will not go well. Fire will come out of these guys' mouths like that of angry dragons and will incinerate their attackers.

People are going to hate these two—not only because of their words, but because they are going to dry up the rain clouds. For three-and-a-half years as they're preaching in Jerusalem, they'll have the power to bring a drought wherever and whenever they feel like it. Finally, at the finish of their mission, the forces of evil will kill them. But even that won't go as planned.

> Now after the three-and-a-half days the breath of life from God entered them, and they stood on their feet, and great fear fell on those who saw them. And they heard a loud voice from heaven saying to them, "Come up here." And they ascended to heaven in a cloud, and their enemies saw them (Revelation 11:11-12).

If you see those two dead guys coming back to life then floating up to heaven, you are most definitely in the tribulation.

There is one more category of supernatural activity, and it is straight out of a modern horror film. When God's judgments come, they will occur over a series of seven seals, seven trumpets, and seven bowls. During the middle series of these events, after the fifth trumpet sounds, the abyss will be unlocked and opened, and what John writes next sends chills up my spine. This abyss, or bottomless pit, is where many of Satan's demons are held for future punishment. When the lid is lifted, demons will pour out—a vast army of them, looking like a swarm of locusts.

> Out of the smoke locusts came upon the earth. And to them was given power, as the scorpions of the earth have power. They were commanded not to harm the grass of the earth, or any green thing, or any tree, but only those men who do not have the seal of God on their foreheads. And they were not given authority to kill them, but to torment them for five months. Their torment was like the torment of a scorpion when it strikes a man. In those days men will seek death and will not find it; they will desire to die, and death will flee from them (Revelation 9:3-6).

For five months, these demonic creatures will torture humanity. It will be horrible. And what you discover about the judgments of Revelation is that as they progress, they do not lighten up or get easier. They only get worse. That's what will happen when the next trumpet, the sixth, is blown. Four demonic angels that have been bound by the Euphrates River for centuries—maybe even millennia—will finally be released. They will go about their business with vengeance and hatred. They will quickly gather an army of 200 million. Are these other demons, or are they people? We aren't told, but their activity seems to indicate they're demons because they spew fire, smoke, and brimstone out of their mouths. They will wreak devastation, killing a third of all humans who are still left alive at the time.

The tribulation will be a time of unprecedented supernatural activity. If you look around and see all these terrible events that can't be explained by natural processes, just know that everything will continue to go downhill.

Wars and Violence

"Wars and violence? Um, Amir, have you looked at the world lately?" Fair enough. Earlier when we looked at the geopolitical state of the world, we saw clearly that the wars and rumors of wars criterion for the onset of the tribulation was certainly being met. The difference, however, between what is happening now and what will take place during the tribulation is that the future will be much, much worse.

Years ago, there was an iconic scene on a television show in which one of the characters wanted to order a "big salad" at a restaurant. Confused, the server asked her to describe what a big salad was. The woman replied, "It's a salad, only bigger." That's how it will be during the tribulation. There are wars now, and during the tribulation, there will be wars, only bigger. In many cities today, there is violence with ever-increasing incidents of murder, assault, kidnapping, and rape. During the tribulation, cities will be filled with even more violence, particularly when you factor in what we will soon learn about food shortages.

When the Lamb of God opens the second seal, a red horse trots forward, "and it was granted to the one who sat on it to take peace from the earth, and that people should kill one another; and there was given to him a great sword" (Revelation 6:4). If you are planning on sticking around through the tribulation and you do not own a firearm, you better get yourself one. As legal systems everywhere break down, violent people will come for what you have. If you want to keep your things, you had better be prepared to defend yourself.

If somehow you make it to the end of the tribulation, you will witness a battle that will be unlike anything the world has ever seen. When the sixth bowl judgment is poured out, the path will be prepared for a demonically summoned army to gather from all over the world in a place called Armageddon. Led by the antichrist, this horde will march against Jerusalem, only to be met by the recently returned Messiah and His army. The slaughter of the enemy will be vast, and the Lord's victory will be assured.

Scarcity and Economic Collapse

When the third seal is opened by the Lamb, a rider will come forward on a black horse. John writes that "he who sat on it had a pair of scales in his hand. And I heard a voice in the midst of the four living creatures saying, 'A quart of wheat for a denarius, and three quarts of barley for a denarius; and do not harm the oil and the wine'" (Revelation 6:5-6). When COVID hit, store shelves emptied. Supply lines were broken due to companies temporarily shutting down and workforces disappearing. It was a difficult time for many. Lines wound through grocery stores and out the front doors as people tried to purchase the basic staples they needed. Eventually, the supply lines were reestablished, although in many places throughout the world, in both developed and developing countries, shortages still remain and empty shelves are a common sight.

Now imagine what it will be like when there is no expectation of those empty shelves being restocked. Picture the mom-and-pop stores, then the big-box retailers, closing their doors because they can't get products to sell. Think of the Great Depression. Recall the unemployment and inflation surrounding the COVID pandemic. Then remember that the tribulation will bring economic collapse, only vastly bigger. There will be fear and violence in the cities, the suburbs, and even the small towns as desperate people band together to hunt door-to-door for food to pass on to their families. You do not want to be around for that.

Death

As of today, more than 6.5 million people have died worldwide from COVID.[31] This is a tragedy of epic proportions, and I in no way want to demean the losses that so many have experienced. Unfortunately, when the tribulation comes, it, too, will have a death toll, only much, much bigger.

> When He opened the fourth seal, I heard the voice of the fourth living creature saying, "Come and see." So I looked, and behold, a pale horse. And the name of him who sat on it was Death, and Hades followed with him. And power was given to them over a fourth of the earth, to kill with sword, with hunger, with death, and by the beasts of the earth (Revelation 6:7-8).

The current world population is 7.98 billion. That means that COVID has killed .08 percent of mankind. When the rider on the pale horse gallops across the earth, he will take 25 percent of the population with him. COVID has taken its 6.5 millions; the tribulation its 2 billions. And notice how the deaths will come. Violence and starvation will take many. The word translated "death" in the above passage means "pestilences," so disease will take many more. And then there will be a large number of people who are attacked and eaten by wild animals, possibly due to the ecological devastation that will accompany many of the judgments.

That slaughter will take place during the seal judgments. The trumpet and bowl judgments are still to come afterward. Remember that when the sixth trumpet is blown, the 200-million-strong demonic army will pour over the earth and kill another third of humanity. When we subtract the initial two billion from the world population, we are left with approximately six billion. One-third of that number means another two billion will be violently slaughtered before the seventh trumpet has a chance to sound.

When you see death tolls add up to half the world's population, you are most definitely in the tribulation.

Diseases

The fourth horseman shows us that disease will kill many in the tribulation. But not all diseases experienced during God's wrath are designed to kill. There is at least one that will be specially created just to cause misery. As the first of the angels of the final series of judgments poured out his bowl, "a foul and loathsome sore came upon the men who had the mark of the beast and those who worshiped his image" (Revelation 16:2). No expiration date is given for these sores, as there was when the stinging locust-looking demons left after five months. When the darkness of the fifth bowl is poured out, people will still be in anguish from these first bowl wounds.

Earthquakes

The earth has long been ravaged by the effects of sin and has been in a state of gradual deterioration. During the tribulation, the Lord will use the fragile state of the globe to bring about natural disasters. But He will also reach down at times with a much more hands-on approach.

According to the US Geological Survey (USGS), the earth shakes around 55 times a day. Most of these quakes are minor, but there are typically 15 each year that break the 7.0 barrier and one that reaches past 8.0.[32] So, during the tribulation, it will not be a surprise when the earth starts shaking. What will catch people's attention is the power of the temblors. Remember, during the tribulation, everything will be bigger.

The first earthquake that we see in the tribulation comes when the sixth seal is opened:

> Behold, there was a great earthquake; and the sun became
> black as sackcloth of hair, and the moon became like
> blood. And the stars of heaven fell to the earth, as a fig
> tree drops its late figs when it is shaken by a mighty wind.

Then the sky receded as a scroll when it is rolled up, and every mountain and island was moved out of its place (Revelation 6:12-14).

Because this earthquake is accompanied by events affecting the sun and the moon, it has been speculated that this could refer to a nuclear explosion or a massive volcanic eruption. Both are certainly possible. It could also be that the damage resulting from the earthquake will cause widespread fires, and the smoke will have an effect on people's perceptions of the sun and the moon.

Revelation describes other tremors throughout the seven years. The earth will shake just before the bowl judgments, when an angel throws to the earth a censer filled with fire from the altar (Revelation 8:5). Jerusalem will lose one-tenth of its buildings when the city shakes following the ascension of the two witnesses (11:13). When the temple in heaven is opened, the residual effects on the earth will be an earthquake and a massive hailstorm (11:19). Then, finally, when the last of God's wrath is expended with the seventh bowl, there will be "a great earthquake, such a mighty and great earthquake as had not occurred since men were on the earth. Now the great city [will be] divided into three parts, and the cities of the nations [will fall]" (16:18-19).

In 2015, Hollywood released a disaster movie entitled *San Andreas*. Starring Dwayne Johnson as a Los Angeles Fire Department helicopter-rescue pilot, the film showed what might happen when the "Big One" hits the San Andreas fault line. The entire coast of California was devastated, and at one point, a massive tsunami slammed into San Francisco, drowning all who weren't able to escape to the upper floors of the city's high-rises. When I watch movies like that, I can't help but think of this final earthquake to end all earthquakes and the global devastation it will cause through the initial shake, the resulting fires and explosions, and the tsunamis that will destroy everything for miles inland.

If you see all the major coastal cities of the world underwater, you are definitely in the tribulation. However, that won't happen until the seventh bowl judgment, so I'm pretty sure you will have figured that out already.

Things Falling from the Skies

If you see fire and giant meteors falling from the skies on a regular basis, you are definitely in the tribulation. As we've already seen, every now and then the false prophet will get the attention of the crowd with fire from heaven. However, when the first trumpet sounds, fire and hail will fall together from the sky. This literal firestorm will be so intense and so widespread that "a third of the trees [will be] burned up, and all green grass [will be] burned up" (8:7). Imagine the number of lives that will be lost, not just through the flames but the overwhelming amount of smoke that will likely kill anyone who has a breathing issue.

When the second trumpet sounds, a "great mountain burning with fire" will be "thrown into the sea, and a third of the sea" will become blood. "And a third of the living creatures in the sea" will die, and a third of the ships will be destroyed (v. 8). This sounds very much like what would happen after a giant meteor strike. But it could also be just what it says—something huge that John couldn't identify but looked like a giant mountain hurled into the sea, causing it to turn into blood. While we often try to find "natural" equivalents for obscure descriptions, we always need to keep in mind that God has an arsenal of supernatural weapons that He can employ whenever He wants.

This giant whatever-it-is will wipe out one-third of all the saltwater marine life and one-third of the ships. The other two-thirds will have a reprieve, but only until the second bowl, when "the second angel poured out his bowl on the sea, and it became blood as of a dead man; and every living creature in the sea died" (16:3).

A similar disaster will occur to the world's fresh water:

> The third angel sounded [his trumpet]: And a great star
> fell from heaven, burning like a torch, and it fell on a
> third of the rivers and on the springs of water. The name
> of the star is Wormwood. A third of the waters became
> wormwood, and many men died from the water, because
> it was made bitter (8:10-11).

One-third of the fresh water will be gone until the pouring of
the third bowl, which will turn the rest of the rivers and streams to
blood. City water systems will be destroyed. Whatever water can be
found will be tainted with deadly poison. And there will be no food
in the grocery stores. Do you have the picture yet that you do not
want to be around for the tribulation?

Contrasting Calamities

This last category sees some contrasting phenomena that God
will employ to carry out His wrath. When the fourth bowl is poured
out, the sun will be given power to scorch people. The original Greek
text means "to torture with intense heat." Whether it is because the
ozone layer has finally given way or the pouring of the bowl on the
sun superheats it, people all over the earth are going to suffer severe
burns from the sun's rays. Yet so deluded will they be by the lies of
the antichrist and the deception of Satan that they still won't repent.
Instead, we see that "they blasphemed the name of God who has
power over these plagues; and they did not repent and give Him
glory" (16:9). They will be so lost and so foolish; don't fall into the
same trap of turning your back on God.

On the flip side of having too much sun, there will be times
when there is too little. When trumpet four sounds, "a third of the
sun [will be] struck, a third of the moon, and a third of the stars, so

that a third of them [will be] darkened. A third of the day [will] not shine, and likewise the night" (8:12). Many people have had difficulties with this passage, saying that if a third of the sun will be darkened, then the earth will freeze. However, when we look at the full context, it appears that rather than the actual celestial entities being damaged, it is their light that will be affected. Thus, 8 hours of the 24-hour day will be plunged into darkness.

This also fits the pattern of the trumpet-to-bowl increases that we see with the waters. While the fourth trumpet will cause one-third of the day to lose its light, the fifth bowl will remove light completely from the world:

> The fifth angel poured out his bowl on the throne of the beast, and his kingdom became full of darkness; and they gnawed their tongues because of the pain. They blasphemed the God of heaven because of their pains and their sores, and did not repent of their deeds (16:10-11).

This darkness will be paralyzing. There will be no flashlights or lanterns to cut through the intense blackness. With sight gone, all the other senses will heighten. It will be a time of terror as every little sound will have you wondering who is creeping up on you. It will be a time of anguish because you won't be able to do anything except sit there and wallow in the pain of your festering sores from the first bowl and your seared flesh from the fourth. But once again, as John told us, rather than turning to God in repentance, people will blaspheme Him in their rebellion.

One final contrast sets the complete windless calm seen at the beginning of Revelation 7 against the powerful hailstorms of 11:19 and 16:21. It is the latter of these storms that will accompany the earthquake to end all earthquakes during the pouring of the seventh bowl. The hailstones will weigh up to 100 pounds. That's the weight of a recliner chair. Imagine a storm with tens of thousands of recliner chairs dropping to the earth at 150 miles per hour. Your umbrella won't help you, nor will the roof of your house. There will be no place to hide from this calamity.

FINAL WORDS

Believe it or not, I hesitated to include this chapter. I don't want to be seen as sensationalizing the tribulation in any way in order to sell more books. However, it is important to understand just how terrible the wrath of God will be. It's more than just a "Yeah, you sure don't want to be around for that" said with a little chuckle. It will be horror beyond imagination. Dear friend, it's true—you do not want to be around when the tribulation begins. Remember, the only reason you would still be here is if you foolishly and rebelliously rejected the free offer of salvation given by God.

Also, if you are reeling from what you have read in this chapter and thinking, *How could God do this?*, let me encourage you to go back and reread chapter 3, where we looked at the heinous nature of sin and the deep mercy of God. Humanity's rebellion against its Creator deserves every ounce of the coming wrath. But God's desire is that no one experience the tribulation. In fact, He wanted so much to spare you from it that Jesus subjected Himself to suffering, torture, and a horrifically violent death just so you could be spared the punishment of your sin. Do not let His sacrifice for you go to waste. Do not open yourself up to the suffering of the tribulation. Choose salvation. Choose hope. Choose Jesus.

WHAT'S MOST IMPORTANT

So, has the tribulation begun? No, it has not. However, by all indications, it is not far away. But even more important than the fact of God's impending wrath drawing ever nearer is the question, "So what?" If I knew that the rapture was going to take place tomorrow or next year or a decade from now, how should I live my life today? And should the primary focus of my life be any different based on a tomorrow rapture compared to a 2032 departure?

THE BELIEVER'S CONTRADICTION

For the Christian, life on this earth is a continuous contradiction. We understand that the world was originally created to be eternal, but humanity's sin irreparably tainted God's perfect creative work. We, too, were tainted by sin, but praise the Lord, the damage to us was not irreparable. From before the beginning of time God had devised a plan for our redemption from the penalty of sin through the sacrifice of His Son:

> You were not redeemed with corruptible things, like silver
> or gold, from your aimless conduct received by tradition

from your fathers, but with the precious blood of Christ, as of a lamb without blemish and without spot. He indeed was foreordained before the foundation of the world, but was manifest in these last times for you who through Him believe in God, who raised Him from the dead and gave Him glory, so that your faith and hope are in God (1 Peter 1:18-21).

God knew we would fall, and He knew how much our reconciliation with Him would cost. Still, His love and His desire for a relationship with us was so great that He deemed the price worth it. This is where our contradiction comes into play.

As Christians, we recognize the immortality of the human soul. We know that we are eternal beings who are living on a temporal planet. This world is not our home; we are here only as ambassadors for Christ. We also recognize that the majority of people in this world don't realize that they, too, are eternal beings. They don't have our long-range perspective. Not recognizing the temporary nature of this planet, they live their lives for the here and now. Sadly, it is only when their time on the earth is done that they will realize the mistake they have made. By then it will be too late.

As immortal souls who recognize our eternality in this temporal home, we must live as fish out of water when it comes to our culture. The "he who dies with the most toys wins" philosophy should hold nothing for us. Money, happiness, and freedom should not rate anywhere near the top of our priority list. Unfortunately, most believers don't live for the eternal in the here and now. They buy into the deception of the temporal to the detriment of that which really matters. Rather than focusing on the mind of Christ, they live the values of the world.

When police officers go out on patrol, they look at the streets very differently than you or I. When we drive from point A to point B, we are usually oblivious to what is going on around us beyond the brake lights of the car we are following. Police officers' eyes, however, are constantly on the move. They are looking in parking lots and down alleys. They are examining the license plates of the vehicles around them while evaluating whether the drivers are adhering to the traffic laws. Compared to our uninterested tunnel vision, they are hyper-aware of their surroundings.

That is how we as believers must be in the world. We must be constantly on the job, always looking for those who need to know the truth. That is because we are on a mission given to us directly from the Messiah:

> All authority has been given to Me in heaven and on earth. Go therefore and make disciples of all the nations, baptizing them in the name of the Father and of the Son and of the Holy Spirit, teaching them to observe all things that I have commanded you; and lo, I am with you always, even to the end of the age (Matthew 28:18-20).

Soon after Jesus gave the disciples this charge, "He was parted from them and carried up into heaven" (Luke 24:51). The disciples didn't know how long it would be before He would return, but they lived as if it was imminent. Again, that word means that He could come at any time. So, after a Holy Spirit boost at Pentecost, these men jumped fully into their roles as spreaders of the gospel. For all but one of them, it would cost their lives—a price they willingly paid.

What was so different about them that they could be that gung-ho about spreading Jesus' message of salvation? Was it that they had seen the Lord? That may be part of it. But there are plenty of examples of believers who have given their lives for the gospel who never laid their physical eyes on the Savior. When it comes down to it, the disciples were no different than you or me. Once the church venerated them as saints, it was as if a gulf was created between them and us. Remember, they were just a bunch of fishermen, blue-collar workers, and a tax collector. What made the difference for them is that they committed to carrying out the mission of Christ no matter the cost. How can we, living in this world of contradiction, also keep our eyes on the eternal rather than the temporal? The answer to that question is where we find the "So what?" of what appears to be our soon-coming departure.

Mission over Comfort

In the Western church, we don't understand persecution. If you want to know what being a Christian can cost you, look to the pastors who are in Iranian jails. Or go to the hidden house churches in China. Or listen to the testimonies of the Nigerian survivors of Boko Haram attacks on their churches. That is true persecution. What we are experiencing in the West is inconvenience. But true persecution is coming for the tribulation believers.

For us now, the worst we will likely experience due to the sharing of our faith is some awkwardness, maybe a few tough questions, and possibly some embarrassment when we aren't sure of the answers. Now that you've read what will happen during the tribulation, do you think those inconveniences are too high of a price to pay for your loved ones to be rescued from the years of God's wrath?

But the problem isn't just that Christians don't want to risk a conflict by sharing their faith. Most don't even think about it! It's not part of their lifestyle. They have bought into the satanic mindset that this life is about them—their comfort, their contentment. As a result, they waste their lives with wasteful living. What is wasteful living? It is all that time, money, and effort focused on yourself and your happiness and your stuff.

When I first became a father, I knew that my life had changed. Seeing my newborn son was one of the most wonderful moments of my life. But with great joy came great responsibility. No longer could I live for myself. I had an obligation to this child to sacrifice whatever was necessary to ensure that he grew up well taken care of.

The same is true when we are reborn. We experience the peace and hope of salvation. Our fear of the future is gone. We rejoice in the fact that we have become children of God and heirs of our Father. But with our great joy comes great responsibility. Paul put it this way:

> By grace you have been saved through faith, and that not of yourselves; it is the gift of God, not of works, lest anyone should boast. For we are His workmanship, created in Christ Jesus for good works, which God prepared beforehand that we should walk in them (Ephesians 2:8-10).

We have been given the free gift of salvation. And we are expected to use it. Being a Christian is more than just possessing a ticket to heaven. When we say yes to Jesus, we are not just becoming part of His family, we are joining up with His workforce. He has created us and called us to Himself, and now He is ready to deploy us to the tasks that He has specially prepared for each of us individually.

The temporal focus says, "I've got to get all the enjoyment I can out of this life now. I've got to see all I can see and do all I can do. I've got to visit all the places I want to go to. My bucket list runneth over, and I've got to check off every item." This is a perfectly understandable mindset if you know nothing about eternity. But we know better. Jesus said,

> If anyone desires to come after Me, let him deny himself, and take up his cross, and follow Me. For whoever desires to save his life will lose it, but whoever loses his life for My sake will find it (Matthew 16:24-25).

Those are familiar words for anyone who has been a Christian for any amount of time. The question is, are you truly living it? Are you denying yourself for the sake of your mission? Are you sacrificing your comfort in pursuit of your calling? There are many Christians who would be willing to die for their faith. But how many are genuinely living it day by day by day? Paul compared our lives to a race, writing, "Do you not know that those who run in a race all run, but one receives the prize? Run in such a way that you may obtain it" (1 Corinthians 9:24). What does it look like to run to win? Look at Paul's life. As his time on this earth was winding down, he wrote:

> I am already being poured out as a drink offering, and the time of my departure is at hand. I have fought the good fight, I have finished the race, I have kept the faith. Finally, there is laid up for me the crown of righteousness, which the Lord, the righteous Judge, will give to me on that Day, and not to me only but also to all who have loved His appearing (2 Timothy 4:6-8).

He ran hard until the end, always mindful that each day could be his last, whether through death or rapture. We must live the same way, because by death or rapture, each day might also be our last. Time is short; don't waste it on yourself.

Unity over Division

I have never seen the church as divided as it is right now. Believers are at each other's throats, arguing over social media, calling each other names, all claiming to be right in the Lord's eyes. The problem is that the issues they are fighting over have nothing to do with doctrine. These are not arguments about the gospel or the finer points of Scripture. This is not a new reformation or a "cleaning of the house" for the church. As far as the major doctrines of the Christian faith go, if we are true believers, we are all in agreement. What is dividing the church lately and causing believers to question one another's salvation has to do with more peripheral matters, such as medical decisions, social issues, and politics.

Sadly, the church is in an age of increased division. But division in the church is nothing new. Even in the first-century church, Paul warned Timothy against those who cause division. In his second letter to his protégé, he warned of those who "strive about words to no profit" (2:14), who speak "profane and idle babblings" (2:16), who participate in "foolish and ignorant disputes" (2:23), and who will have "itching ears" and "turn their ears away from the truth, and be turned aside to fables" (4:3-4). Looking at that list, you'd almost think that Paul had Facebook!

I've seen division over blood moons and *shmita*. People have torn each other apart over 9/11 conspiracy theories and red heifers. Every now and then I will look at the comments that are made during my live video updates and while a vast majority are very encouraging and made by truly wonderful people, others have left me shaking my head. I learn about beliefs that I never knew I held, and I read about things I have said that I would never in my life say. All this saddens me, because I see Satan's foothold in the church on display within the comments of my very own videos.

There are millions of people who need to know the simple, pure gospel of Jesus Christ. Conspiracy theories are not what is going to lead them to the truth. Your love and self-sacrificing service toward them will. Actually, even more than that, it is our love and self-sacrificing service toward each other that will help lead people to the truth. What did Jesus say about the need for our unity?

> A new commandment I give to you, that you love one another; as I have loved you, that you also love one another.

> By this all will know that you are My disciples, if you have
> love for one another (John 13:34-35).

Genuine sacrificial love is very rare these days, particularly outside the family unit. When people see true love being put into practice, it is appealing and will draw them in like flies to honey. Let's make that the hallmark of our in-person and online discussions with one another.

I'm not saying to stop believing what it is you believe. If you and your pastor can back up your convictions biblically, more power to you. What I am saying is to stop attacking fellow believers who may not agree with you on nonessentials. Quit the trolling. Stop the sniping. Instead of using this time to attack one another with memes, use it to encourage each other and study the Word of God. Let joy overcome anger and unity overwhelm division.

The time is short and gets shorter every day. Meanwhile, Satan laughs because of the wedge he's driven into the church through distraction, dissension, vitriol, and confusion. We are on a mission in the time we have left. Let's put aside the "them versus us" when it comes to issues that have nothing to do with the gospel. Instead, if there is anything that people are going to see in us, let it be love, unity, and the light of hope and peace that comes through a relationship with our Lord and Savior, Jesus.

Christ over Everything Else

Jesus is coming back soon!

Just let that truth sink in. When we compare Scripture with what we see in the world around us, we can say without hesitation or exaggeration that the rapture could happen today and the tribulation will soon follow. But even should the Lord tarry for a few years or a few decades, we all know that it won't be long before our time on this earth is done and we are in the presence of our God. In the remaining time left, whether it be hours or years, what are you going to do?

My dear friend, there is no more worthy way to spend that shrinking gap between now and forever than fulfilling your mission as an ambassador for Christ. In your home, in your workplace, in your church, in your neighborhood, be a light that shows people that there is hope in this deteriorating world. Let them see that peace can be had in our divided, violent culture. Tell them that worse times are coming, but that they don't need to be afraid. Jesus is coming to take those who belong to Him, and all they need to do to be part of that rescue operation is to believe and receive the free gift of salvation.

That is why you are here.

No, the tribulation has not begun. But it is coming on fast. Are you ready?

Jesus told a parable of ten virgins who took their lamps and went out to wait for the coming bridegroom. Five of them were smart and brought along oil for their lamps. Five were distracted by other things and didn't think to pack some oil. When the cry came at midnight that the bridegroom was coming, the five foolish women suddenly realized their mistake. Panicked, they asked for help from the wise virgins, who unfortunately had enough only for themselves. In a rush, the foolish five left to buy some oil of their own.

> And while they went to buy, the bridegroom came, and those who were ready went in with him to the wedding; and the door was shut. Afterward the other virgins came also, saying, "Lord, Lord, open to us!" But he answered and said, "Assuredly, I say to you, I do not know you." Watch therefore, for you know neither the day nor the hour in which the Son of Man is coming (Matthew 25:10-13).

I often wonder what might have happened if one of the wise virgins had said to the foolish ones, "Hey, ladies, you may want to get some oil so that you're ready for when the bridegroom comes." They may have ignored her or even ridiculed her, saying, "What are you so worried about? We'll have plenty of time." But maybe one or two would have listened, gotten their oil, and made it through the door.

NOW IS THE TIME

The window of opportunity to escape the coming tribulation is closing. Don't let anything distract you from readying yourself or from letting your loved ones know that now is the time to grab the oil. Now is the time to prepare your heart.

> We then, as workers together with Him also plead with you not to receive the grace of God in vain. For He says:
>
> "In an acceptable time I have heard you,
>   and in the day of salvation I have helped you."
>
> Behold, now is the accepted time; behold, now is the day of salvation (2 Corinthians 6:1-2).

NOTES

1. "Immigration by Country 2022," *World Population Review*, https://worldpopulationreview.com/country-rankings/immigration-by-country.

2. "Many Americans Say Other Faiths Can Lead to Eternal Life," *Pew Research Center*, December 18, 2008, https://www.pewresearch.org/religion/2008/12/18/many-americans-say-other-faiths-can-lead-to-eternal-life/.

3. "Apostolic Journey of His Holiness Pope Francis to the United Arab Emirates," PDF download, https://www.vatican.va/content/francesco/en/travels/2019/outside/documents/papa-francesco_20190204_documento-fratellanza-umana.html.

4. Ibid.

5. "John Paul II: General Audience," December 6, 2000, PDF download, https://www.vatican.va/content/john-paul-ii/en/audiences/2000/documents/hf_jp-ii_aud_20001206.html.

6. Mark Lungariello, "Pastor threatens to kick out mask-wearing worshippers from church," *New York Post*, July 27, 2021, https://nypost.com/2021/07/27/pastor-threatens-to-kick-out-mask-wearing-worshippers/.

7. Justin Taylor, "9 Reasons We Can Be Confident Christians Won't Be Raptured Before the Tribulation," *TGC*, August 5, 2014, https://www.thegospelcoalition.org/blogs/justin-taylor/9-reasons-we-can-be-confident-christians-wont-be-raptured-before-the-tribulation/.

8. John Piper, "Definitions and Observations Concerning the Second Coming of Christ," *Desiring God*, August 30, 1987, https://www.desiringgod.org/articles/definitions-and-observations-concerning-the-second-coming-of-christ.

9. "U.S. Antisemitic Incidents Remained at Historic High in 2020," *ADL*, April 26, 2021, https://www.adl.org/resources/press-release/us-antisemitic-incidents-remained-historic-high-2020.

10. Cnaan Liphshiz, "European Jews worry war against antisemitism has been lost," *Jewish Journal*, June 3, 2021, https://www.sun-sentinel.com/florida-jewish-journal/fl-jj-european-jews-worry-war-against-antisemitism-lost-20210603-wjtwl4mvznen5f3eleovkxii3i-story.html.

11. "G.W.F. Hegel 1770–1831," *Oxford Reference*, https://www.oxfordreference.com/view/10.1093/acref/9780191826719.001.0001/q-oro-ed4-00005305.

12. Eric Snow, "The Life Cycles of Empires," *Beyond Today*, July 6, 2011, https://www.ucg.org/the-good-news/the-life-cycles-of-empires-lessons-for-america-today.

13. "Imminent," *Merriam-Webster*, https://www.merriam-webster.com/dictionary/imminent.

14. "IAEA 'cannot assure' Iran nuke program peaceful; Tehran has enough material for bomb," *The Times of Israel*, September 7, 2022, https://www.timesofisrael.com/un-watchdog-says-it-cannot-assure-irans-nuclear-program-is-peaceful/.

15. Gabriel Honrada, "Iran looks to Russia for Su-35 fighter jet deal," *Asia Times*, September 7, 2022, https://asiatimes.com/2022/09/iran-looks-to-russia-for-su-35-fighter-jet-deal/.

16. "Turkey reaffirms support to Libya's efforts for reconciliation," *Daily Sabah*, February 20, 2022, https://www.dailysabah.com/politics/diplomacy/turkey-reaffirms-support-to-libyas-efforts-for-reconciliation.

17. "Hunger Hotspots: 4 countries face famine, UN report warns," *World Food Programme*, January 28, 2022, https://www.wfp.org/stories/hunger-hotspots-4-countries-face-famine-un-report-warns.

18. "7 reasons why there has been an increase in the number of earthquakes," *Times of India*, December 11, 2017, https://timesofindia.indiatimes.com/home/science/7-reasons-why-there-has-been-an-increase-in-number-of-earthquakes/articleshow/62019578.cms.

19. "Worldwide Surge in 'Great' Earthquakes Seen in Past 10 Years," *NBC News*, updated October 25, 2014, https://www.nbcnews.com/science/science-news/worldwide-surge-great-earthquakes-seen-past-10-years-n233661.

20. Umair Irfan, "We know where the next big earthquakes will happen—but not when," *Vox*, updated January 23, 2018, https://www.vox.com/energy-and-environment/2017/9/21/16339522/8-things-to-know-about-earthquakes-alaska.

21. Kathryn Schulz, "The Really Big One," *The New Yorker*, July 13, 2015, https://www.newyorker.com/magazine/2015/07/20/the-really-big-one.

22. "Factbox: Wildfires breaking out across the world," *Reuters*, August 24, 2022, https://www.reuters.com/world/europe/wildfires-breaking-out-across-world-2022-07-19/.

23. "UN chief views 'unimaginable' damage in visit to Pakistan's flood-hit areas," *The Guardian*, September 10, 2022, https://www.theguardian.com/world/2022/sep/10/un-secretary-general-antonio-guterres-pakistan-floods-visit.

24. "Facts and figures on life in the European Union," *European Union*, https://european-union.europa.eu/principles-countries-history/key-facts-and-figures/life-eu_en#:~:text=Size%20and%20population,country%20and%20Malta%20the%20smallest.

25. "What does it mean that the euro has fallen below parity with the dollar?" *PBS News Hour*, August 23, 2022, https://www.pbs.org/newshour/economy/ask-the-headhunter/what-does-it-mean-that-the-euro-has-fallen-below-parity-with-the-dollar.

26. Drew Desilver, "In the U.S. and around the world, inflation is high and getting higher," *Pew Research Center*, June 15, 2022, https://www.pewresearch.org/fact-tank/2022/06/15/in-the-u-s-and-around-the-world-inflation-is-high-and-getting-higher/.

27. Freeman Dyson, "The Question of Global Warming," *The New York Book Review*, June 12, 2008, https://www.nybooks.com/articles/2008/06/12/the-question-of-global-warming/?lp_txn_id=1378152.

28. Henno Kruger, "30 of the Best Jeff Foxworthy 'You Might Be a Redneck' Quotes," *Running Wolf's Rant*, November 1, 2018, https://rwrant.co.za/jeff-foxworthy-you-might-be-a-redneck-quotes/.

29. John C Lennox, *Against the Flow* (Oxford, UK: Lion Hudson, 2015), 259.

30. James Romero, "Images: 10 incredible volcanoes in our solar system," *Space.com*, May 1, 2021, https://www.space.com/incredible-volcanoes-in-our-solar-system.

31. "Coronavirus Death Toll," *worldometer*, October 13, 2022, https://www.worldometers.info/coronavirus/coronavirus-death-toll/.

32. "Why are we having so many earthquakes?," *USGS.gov*, https://www.usgs.gov/faqs/why-are-we-having-so-many-earthquakes-has-naturally-occurring-earthquake-activity-been.

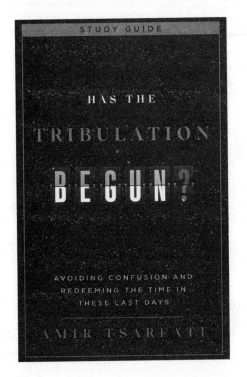

With this study guide companion to *Has the Tribulation Begun?*, bestselling author and prophecy expert Amir Tsarfati guides you through a biblical overview of the last days. The thought-provoking questions within will help you...

- separate Scripture's teaching from popular misconceptions about the end times

- identify if and how today's current events correlate with tribulation precursors

- navigate your life today with an eternal outlook guiding your decisions

Amir Tsarfati, with Dr. Rick Yohn, examines what Revelation makes known about the end times and beyond. Guided by accessible teaching that lets Scripture speak for itself, you'll see what lies ahead for every person in the end times—either in heaven or on earth. Are *you* ready?

This companion workbook to *Revealing Revelation*— the product of many years of careful research—offers you a clear and exciting overview of God's perfect plan for the future. Inside you'll find principles from the Bible that equip you to better interpret the end-times signs, as well as insights about how Bible prophecy is relevant to your life today.

In *Israel and the Church*, bestselling author and native Israeli Amir Tsarfati helps readers recognize the distinct contemporary and future roles of both the Jewish people and the church, and how together they reveal the character of God and His perfect plan of salvation.

To fully grasp what God has in store for the future, it's vital to understand His promises to Israel. The *Israel and the Church Study Guide* will help you do exactly that, equipping you to explore the Bible's many revelations about what is yet to come.

As a native Israeli of Jewish roots, Amir Tsarfati provides a distinct perspective that weaves biblical history, current events, and Bible prophecy together to shine light on the mysteries about the end times. In *The Day Approaching*, he points to the scriptural evidence that the return of the Lord is imminent.

Jesus Himself revealed the signs that will alert us to the nearness of His return. In *The Day Approaching Study Guide*, you'll have the opportunity to take an up-close look at what those signs are, as well as God's overarching plans for the future, and how those plans affect you today.

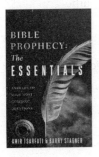

AMIR TSARFATI WITH BARRY STAGNER

In *Bible Prophecy: The Essentials*, Amir and Barry team up to answer 70 of their most commonly asked questions. Through succinct, Scripture-focused teachings, Amir and Barry address seven foundational themes of Bible prophecy: Israel, the church, the rapture, the tribulation, the millennium, the Great White Throne judgment, and heaven.

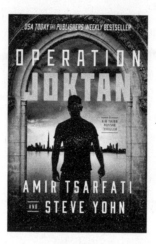

BOOK 1

"It was the perfect day—until the gunfire."

Nir Tavor is an Israeli secret service operative turned talented Mossad agent.

Nicole le Roux is a model with a hidden skill.

A terrorist attack brings them together, and then work forces them apart—until they're unexpectedly called back into each other's lives.

But there's no time for romance. As violent radicals threaten chaos across the Middle East, the two must work together to stop these extremists, pooling Nicole's knack for technology and Nir's adeptness with on-the-ground missions. Each heart-racing step of their operation gets them closer to the truth—and closer to danger.

In this thrilling first book in a new series, authors Amir Tsarfati and Steve Yohn draw on true events as well as tactical insights Amir learned from his time in the Israeli Defense Forces. For believers in God's life-changing promises, *Operation Joktan* is a suspense-filled page-turner that illuminates the blessing Israel is to the world.

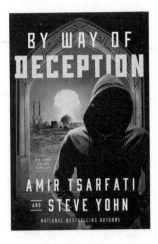

BOOK 2

The Mossad has uncovered Iran's plans to smuggle untraceable weapons of mass destruction into Israel. The clock is ticking, and agents Nir Tavor and Nicole le Roux can't act quickly enough.

Nir and Nicole find themselves caught in a whirlwind plot of assassinations, espionage, and undercover recon, fighting against the clock to stop this threat against the Middle East. As they draw closer to danger—and closer to each other—they find themselves ensnared in a lethal web of secrets. Will they have to sacrifice their own lives to protect the lives of millions?

Inspired by real events, authors Amir Tsarfati and Steve Yohn reteam for this suspenseful follow-up to the bestselling *Operation Joktan*. Filled with danger, romance, and international intrigue, this Nir Tavor thriller reveals breathtaking true insights into the lives and duties of Mossad agents—and delivers a story that will have you on the edge of your seat.

To learn more about our Harvest Prophecy resources, please visit:

www.HarvestProphecyHQ.com

HARVEST PROPHECY
AN IMPRINT OF HARVEST HOUSE PUBLISHERS